D1400090

Mysteries and Miracles
of Colorado

By Jack Kutz

Rhombus Publishing Company

Cover design and illustrations
by Mary Robert

Rhombus Publishing Company, Inc.
P.O. Box 806, Corrales, New Mexico 87048

To Ter

and the Fourteeners we stood on

Contents

Foreword

Colorado. It soars, and it plunges. It glows in autumn, glitters in winter, sings in the night and rises majestically toward each new dawn. Colorado's high country recreates itself each day. It can appear as a sunny Elysium paradise one moment and a dark, forbidding Tolkien Mordor the next.

If there was ever a mystical mountain kingdom where reality and fantasy intertwine, where mysterious and miraculous events constantly occur, it is Colorado. Colorado continuously casts a spell; sometimes it is a blessing, sometimes a curse. But it has affected many Coloradans' lives in dramatic, romantic and often tragic ways.

The strange events that have taken place across this wondrous state have been somewhat neglected by historians, perhaps because many of these stories are very difficult to believe, and cannot be satisfactorily explained. But widely scattered references to these arcane happenings and to the lives of the star-crossed people who experienced them do exist. Bits and pieces of the original stories can be found if one is a diligent searcher, willing to delve and dig deeply into the right places where these obscure facts are tucked away.

Since I began my series of books on the mysteries and miracles of the American Southwest a few years ago, searching for these lost tales has become one of my greatest fascinations and most pleasurable challenges. I have been continuously surprised to find that none of these captivating stories —from the oldest mysteries to the most modern ones— has ever been told in its entirety by a single source.

It took a great deal of cross-referencing to make sure all the facts had been collected, and that each story was complete and accurate. My work took me to many of Colorado's most intriguing out-of-the-way places, to misty, old cemeteries, aged *moradas* and the narrow corridors of a haunted hotel. These and other sites are places which the reader may also visit since, whenever possible, I have given detailed directions for reaching them.

Colorado is a land where skeletons walk at night, candles float in the darkness, and ghostly voices are heard in the twilight. It can be an eerie realm within which strange lights appear where no lights should be —in the black, star-filled sky and on the mountain tops, in the deep, dense forests and in the wind-swept grass around one's feet. Yet not all of Colorado's mysteries are supernatural or other-worldly. Some of the stories in this book can probably be classified simply as exceptionally dramatic true-life crime stories, tales of vengeance, utter desperation or unprincipled greed.

This collection of tales covers scores of strange, baffling events. Some of the mysteries have been solved, others have not, and some never will be. But

together they give us rare glimpses of astonishing phenomena far beyond our current ability to understand.

I welcome you to the Surreal Colorado.

1

The Granby Idol

It was the damnedest rock Bud Chalmers had ever seen. When he brushed the dirt off, it grinned at him.

Chalmers found the rock on his little homestead in the beautiful, alpine country northeast of Granby. He was a hard-working man who had already dug up more than his fair share of rocks while shaping his small piece of land into a successful ranch. During the summer of 1920, his primary project was the construction of a pond-sized reservoir which would use some of the water flowing down a shallow tributary of the Colorado River's south fork.

He used a team of horses to drag a scraper across the ground, and then he tossed the scooped up rocks onto the circular embankment he was building around his reservoir. Chalmers worked at a near-rhythmic pace, wasting no energy as he hefted and threw each of the rocks. From past experience, he knew by the size and weight of each rock how much effort would be needed to hoist it up, fling it away and turn back to grab the next one. Halfway through the emptying of one of those scraper-loads, he started to toss a rock, paused in mid-swing, and let it drop to the ground.

The rock was heavier than it should have been. It was not a very large stone; later it would be measured at 16 inches tall and 12 inches across at its broadest part. After cleaning it off, Chalmers saw that the rock was dark colored, almost black when compared to typical grey Colorado granite. It was as smooth as a river stone, and ...it had been sculpted.

On the top of the stone, a face had been chiseled. The face was a jolly one, with a wide, toothy smile which squinched up the eyes above it. Alongside the face were large elfin ears; below that, three-fingered hands clasped the figure's sides. On its flat tummy, a hodge-podge of strange symbols had been carved.

Odder still were the bas-relief carvings on the back of the stone. A prehistoric hairy mammoth was depicted while on the left side, a long-necked dinosaur stretched out and rested its head on the idol's brow. The bottom of the rock was perfectly flat so that when it was placed on a level surface, it squatted solidly and beamed its merry smile at anyone who came to look at it.

Quite a few people did come to look at this curi-

THE GRANBY IDOL. These photographs are the only known proof that the stone existed. It measured 16 inches tall by 12 inches wide.

ous artifact after Bud Chalmers carried it up to his house and plunked it on his porch. He invited his neighbors over and asked what they thought it might be, and where it could have come from. All his friends did was shrug their shoulders.

One area resident who took a particular interest in the rock was Lela Smith, the local schoolteacher. Smith taught all of the children in this isolated region from a one room log cabin known as the Sleepy Hollow School. Her students rode in on horseback from ranches whenever weather permitted. Smith boarded at the ramshackle Cold Springs Ranch, two miles from the schoolhouse.

This ranch was only a short distance from Chalmers' place, so one Sunday she rode down to see the "laughing boulder" that all the children were talking about.

Lela Smith was so amazed by this peculiar object that she remounted her horse and galloped back to Cold Springs to pick up her box camera. With the afternoon sun bright upon the stone, she photographed it from several different angles. Had it not been for Smith's photographs, the existence of the Granby Idol might well be forgotten today.

Within a year or two, Bud Chalmers gave the rock to his son who stored it in his garage in Granby. Occasionally, people still dropped by to look at the oddity, but interest was waning until in 1926, a man named Henry F. Knight viewed the stone.

Knight was an outsider to the scattered rural community around Granby. He was a monied man from St. Louis who enjoyed vacationing in the West. He had become so enamored of the idyllic Granby countryside that he had purchased a ranch north of the Chalmers spread in 1926.

After closely examining the idol, Knight told Chalmers, "Bud, this artifact belongs in a museum, not in a garage. If you want to sell it, I'll give you $300 for it." To a hard-working rancher like Bud Chalmers, that was a pretty darn good price for a rock, so he sold it. Reportedly, Knight donated it to a museum somewhere "back East." No one in Colorado ever saw the stone again.

Forty three years went by and then in 1969, an article, "Runestones and Tombstones," appeared in *Old West* magazine. In the article, Lela Smith Mac-Quary, now an elderly woman residing in Denver, recounted the story of the Granby Idol. Two of *Old West's* readers, Bernice and Jack McGee, had a long-standing interest in out-of-place artifacts ("ooparts", as they are sometimes called). They contacted the retired school teacher and were delighted to learn she had kept her photographs all those years. They were even happier when she unhesitatingly agreed to loan the pictures for study by experts.

The McGees compared the idol's belly inscriptions with their own personal file of archaic scripts; they found nothing that matched, but they had a hunch. They sent the photos on to Dr. Cyclone Covey, a professor of Ancient and Colonial History, and the author of *Ancient Chinese Sojourns in America*. Dr. Covey took one long look at the inscription and probably shouted, "This is it! This is exactly what I've been looking for!" Without delay, he called the McGees in to inform them that the inscription was Chinese ...not the stylized Chinese of today, but rather the more crude symbols that were in use more than 1,000 years ago.

Covey firmly believed the ancient Chinese made trans-Pacific voyages to the western hemisphere earlier than the trans-Atlantic crossings of the Vikings and the Mediterranean peoples. The primary obstacle in proving his theories had been the lack of any artifactual evidence of their presence on this continent.

True, there was plenty of evidence of an Oriental influence in the artwork of the Mayans, the Incas and the early Mexican civilizations. Many clay figurines of Mayan deities look surprisingly Buddhist. Carvings of Mayan serpents are strikingly similar to ancient depictions of Chinese sea monsters and dragons. The Asian "cosmic tree" with a demonic face showing through its branches is nearly identical to stone friezes found in Mesoamerican ruins. Flutes, decorations on terracotta pottery, even children's toys seem so obviously inspired by Oriental cultures that it is hard to dismiss them as coincidental.

Proponents of the theory that the Chinese and Japanese traveled, perhaps frequently, to the Americas are based primarily on the chronicles of Hui-Shen, a Buddhist priest who sailed eastward from China in the Fifth Century A.D. to a distant land he called the kingdom of Fu-Sang. According to Hui-Shen, Fu-Sang was located 20,000 *li* (approximately 6,600 miles) beyond mainland China. It was lush land, rich with fruit where a peaceful people spun thread and made paper from the bark of trees. "They have no fortresses or walled cities," Hui-Shen wrote. "They do not wage war in that kingdom."

Interestingly, Hi-Shen claimed he had followed the route of a much earlier Chinese explorer, an extraordinarily man named Yu. In 2200 B.C. Yu had written a series of manuscripts describing his odyssey to "a land beyond the seas." Yu had a flair for poetry; he tended to exaggerate quite a bit when he spun tales about the wonders he had seen. He swore that in the land he discovered trees soared up one thousand feet into the sky. He also described a "Great Luminous Canyon" so deep no one could see its bottom.

Exaggerations aside, it seems clear that both of these intrepid men, Yu and Hui-Shen, had sailed off into uncharted waters, landed on a far-away shore and returned to tell about it. Just where in the world did they actually go? Was it even remotely possible they crossed the Pacific Ocean?

Thor Heyerdahl of *Kon Tiki* fame knew from personal experience that "oceans have pathways as alive as rivers." He contended that seafarers from the Orient could have ridden to North America on the "Westerlies", the North Pacific Current. They could then have sailed south along the coastline on the California Current, going as far as Latin America on the Peru Current. To return, the Southeast Trade Winds would have carried the aboriginal crafts to Hawaii. From there, the Northeast Trade Winds would have taken them back home.

Voyages of this sort were far from impossible given the skill of the ancient Chinese mariners. But whether or not such journeys actually did take place remained theoretical because not one single antiquated object of provable Chinese origin had ever been found in the Americas. Covey and several of his colleagues felt Smith-MacQuary's photos at last provided proof that at least one such artifact existed.

Four years later, in 1973, hundreds of miles from the Colorado high country, an amazing discovery was made off the coast of California. A United States Geological Survey team was dredging the ocean floor in the Santa Barbara Channel, south of Point Conception when they brought up a doughnut-shaped stone, thirteen inches across and six inches thick, with a two-and-a half-inch hole through its center. It was obviously an out-of-place artifact of some sort.

The Scripps Institute of Oceanography at La Jolla analyzed the stone and found it to be fine-grained dolomite, a type of rock rarely found in California's coastal waters, but quite common in northern China. The stone was also coated with a three-millimeter thick layer of manganese which can take 3,000 years to form under conditions at the bottom of the sea.

Several local sports divers began exploring the area, discovering an assortment of similar handcrafted stones scattered within 300 feet of each other on the sandy ocean floor. The stones ranged in weight from 50 pounds to 1,200 pounds. The Scripps Institute experts hypothesized that the biggest "doughnut" was a ship's anchor while the smaller ones were used to secure mooring lines and riggings. Altogether, 20 stones were recovered and it seemed a safe assumption that they were remnants of a very old shipwreck. Since the Chinese had used stone anchors and weight balancing devices of exactly this type, there was a high probability that the ship had been Chinese.

Not everyone was convinced the artifacts originated in China, of course. Skeptics pointed out that the number of Chinese fishing villages existed up and down the California coast during the mid-1800s. Surely, it was one of their vessels that had sunk. Proponents of the "ancient Chinese mariners" theory countered by noting that none of these fishing boats was capable of carrying or even needing a 1,200-pound anchor.

With the antiquity of the anchor stones unresolved, it seemed that the Granby Idol might be the only real proof of pre-Colombian Chinese explorations in the American West. But even if this strange stone is accepted as a genuine Chinese relic, the riddle of its meaning and purpose only deepens. First, one must contemplate the reasons for its placement. Why was this carved rock deposited so far inland? Was it placed deliberately, or just by accident?

Dr. Cyclone Covey believed the stone may have been a directional aid, a travel marker similar to a contemporary "You Are Here" sign. After Covey identified the inscription as Shang linear characters, he managed to translate most of them. He found the symbols for "north," "river," "fruit" and "fish." He concluded the stone was meant as a guide for future travelers. If so, it might well have been one of a series of such markers blazing a trail across the land.

Perhaps that explains the reason for the stone's existence, but there seems to be no way to account for its most baffling features. Why were depictions of a mammoth and a dinosaur embossed upon the stone?

The mammoth figure is not at all clearly visible in the photograph; Covey had to pretty much take Smith-MacQuary's word for it. But the other figure, on the well-lit left side of the artifact, the depiction of a dinosaur seems unmistakable. It bears no resemblance to a Chinese dragon nor to any type of modern-day lizard.

The creature's long neck gives it the appearance of a reptile from the Jurassic Period, a time some 150 million years ago when great herds of brontosaurs roamed the earth. No human being ever saw a brontosaurus or its cousins, the brachiosaurus and diplodocus. Less than 200 years have passed since a handful of scientists and scholars realized that the fossilized fragments of these extinct reptiles could be pieced together to restore their skeletons. It was absolutely impossible for Yu or Hui-Shen or any other early Chinese explorer to have known of the existence of these prehistoric beasts. How then can it be that a message written in 1,000-year-old Chinese characters, an image of a 150,000,000-year-old dinosaur and a Cro-Magnon era mammoth all appear on the same stone?

Both Yu and Hui-Shen were wise and learned men with mystic and visionary minds. Could it possibly be that they were able to not only explore the outer limits of the world within which they lived, but were also somehow capable of seeing the world as it was in the past?

An extensive archaeological dig on the Chalmers ranch might have yielded more clues, but that opportunity was missed and is now impossible. Today, Granby Lake covers the entire site. In 1946, when construction of the Granby dam began, the local residents asked the Bureau of Reclamation to conduct an archaeological exploration of the Chalmers' property before it was too late. The bureau did a half-hearted survey over about 150 square feet of the property and found nothing. The dam went in and the entire area was permanently flooded.

If the jolly, "laughing boulder" had any stony little pals scattered around him, they are lost forever. Even the whereabouts of the Granby Idol itself is uncertain. Somewhere, in a museum far from Colorado —perhaps in the back of a neglected showcase or even in a packing crate in a basement storage room— the idol sits beaming its eternal smile.

How to Visit Granby Lake

Granby Lake can be reached by Highway 34, eleven miles north of the town of Granby, 60 miles west and north of Idaho Springs. Here, on the edge of one of Colorado's most gloriously scenic areas, Rocky Moun-

tain National Park, sports boats skim the waters cover-
ing the find-site of the long lost Granby Idol.

Bibliography - Chapter 1

Davies, Nigel. **Voyagers to the New World.** Albuquer-
que. University of New Mexico.

Gardener, Joseph L., Project Editor. **Mysteries of the
Ancient Americas.** Pleasantville, New York. The
Reader's Digest Association.

McGee, Bernice and Jack. *True West* magazine. Austin,
Texas. Western Publications, Inc. November-
December, 1971.

McGinty, Brian. *American West* magazine. Buffalo Bill
Historical Center. November-December, 1983.

2

The Lives of Bridey Murphy

Morey Bernstein did *not* believe in hypnosis. To him, it was foolishness, a "silly business," an insult to his intelligence. Once during his college days, some of his friends persuaded him to attend a stage demonstration of hypnosis; midway through the performance he walked out in disgust. "If you want to waste your time watching this, well and fine," he told his companions. "But this is not for me."

At that point in his life, Morey Bernstein had no way of knowing that within just a few years he would become the most famous amateur hypnotist in America.

Bernstein was a prominent businessman in Pueblo, Colorado, a partner in a family-owned enterprise called Bernstein Brothers Equipment Company. He and his wife, Hazel, were a popular, young couple who were frequently invited to cocktail parties in the homes of Pueblo's other aspiring suburbanites. One rainy night in 1950, the Bernsteins joined a small circle of friends who had gathered for an evening of cheese dip, martinis and conversation.

A newcomer turned up in the crowd that night, a young man from Denver passing through on a business trip. He was an amiable fellow who was immediately accepted and asked the usual questions: his family, his job and his spare-time activities. He surprised everyone by saying his hobby was hypnotism. No one took him seriously, so he offered to demonstrate his ability if anyone present was willing to be a subject.

A tall, blonde woman volunteered. The hypnotist, Jerry Thomas, asked her to lie comfortably on the sofa. She did so with just the scantiest apprehension. Thomas took a ring from his finger and held it close to her eyes. "Stare at this ring until it becomes hazy and blurred," he said softly. "Relax. Concentrate your mind on nothing but the ring."

The young woman gazed steadily at the motionless ring. Before long, her eyelids lowered a bit, but beyond that, she seemed to be undergoing no change. Several long minutes went by in the silent room. The party guests grew bored; most of them, including Morey Bernstein, drifted out to the buffet table in the kitchen. "Who is this character?" they whispered among themselves. "He sure is a party-pooper." Then, they heard Thomas begin to talk in a calm, low tone of voice. Bernstein glanced into the living room. The woman appeared to be sleeping contentedly while the hypnotist spoke to her. Though Bernstein listened intently, he could not quite hear Thomas' words. Slowly the man put his ring back on and joined the others in the kitchen.

"She is sleeping peacefully," he said. "I'm going back and gently awaken her. She'll come into the kitchen and sit down to eat some food. After she's

THE REINCARNATION OF BRIDEY MURPHY. Virginia Tighe as a teenager before moving to Colorado.

taken two bites, she will reach down and remove her left shoe."

"Oh, sure she will," Bernstein scoffed.

Jerry Thomas returned to the living room, knelt by the sofa, and spoke again to the sleeping woman. She sat up, and looking somewhat dreamy-eyed, rose to her feet and walked into the kitchen. She smiled at everyone, sat down and dished up some food. As she chewed her second bite, she suddenly dropped her fork, pushed back her chair, and pulled off her left shoe.

Everyone gasped audibly. Her fiance blurted out, "Honey, why did you do that?"

She stared at the shoe in her hand as if she had never seen it before. "I... I don't know," she said, confused.

"Aw, c'mon, Jerry," Bernstein laughed. "No one here's going to fall for a gag like that. You put her up to it; the two of you are just trying to pull off a dumb party joke."

"I don't blame you for being skeptical," Thomas said. "I once felt the same way myself. But if you want further proof, I can put her under again... that is, if she's willing."

She hesitated, then gave a why not? shrug. The hypnotist snapped his fingers three times in front of her face. Instantly, her expression went blank. Her eyes became as immobile as the eyes of a statue.

"This," Jerry Thomas explained, "is known as post-hypnotic suggestion. While she was in her first trance, I suggested that after she awoke, she could return to her trance-state if I snapped my fingers three times."

By now, the fiance was understandably nervous. He stepped up to his bride-to-be and waved his hand back and forth in front of her eyes. She did not blink. He made funny faces at her, trying to make her laugh. She remained totally impassive. Thomas asked the party's hostess to bring him a needle from her sewing basket. When the item was delivered, he lifted the hypnotized woman's hand and pushed the point of the needle into her palm. She did not flinch.

Morey Bernstein plunked down into one of the chrome-legged kitchen chairs, utterly amazed. "Wake her up. I believe you, " he said.

Later, as the Bernsteins drove home through the rain, the windshield wipers slapped rhythmically back and forth. He seemed intensely lost in thoughts until he blurted out. "How did he do it? He proved hypnosis is a reality. Its possibilities are infinite. I've got to learn how it's done!"

The next day, Bernstein called a local bookstore to order every available book on the subject of hypnotism. After work, he went to the public library and walked out with an armload of books. He read far into the night. For weeks, he immersed himself in the techniques of trance induction, therapeutic hypnosis, autosuggestion and, most significantly, age-regression hypnosis.

At last he felt confident enough. "I think I'm ready to try it. If only I could find a subject," he told his wife.

"You might start with me," said Hazel. "I've got another of my migraines. Maybe this hypnotic stuff would help."

Suddenly feeling less sure of himself, Morey asked his wife to lie down on the davenport and relax. He sat on the floor beside her and removed a cuff link from his shirt sleeve. Holding it in front of her face, he asked her to stare at it, giving it her total concentration. In a soothing voice, he told her she was becoming very drowsy, very sleepy. Hazel's eyes soon closed and Morey set the cuff link on the coffee table.

He placed his fingers on her temples and in a voice just above a whisper said, "Your headache is gone. It's gone. You will never have another. Ever." He paused, then repeated his words. He waited a minute and said, "You can awaken now, Hazel. You can awaken." Hazel Bernstein opened her eyes and sat up.

"How do you feel?" he asked. Her smile told him her headache was truly gone and quite possibly might never return.

At that moment, Morey probably felt even better than Hazel did; his first attempt at hypnosis had been a success. After Hazel told her friends about her husband's newly acquired talent, Morey found he had no shortage of willing subjects. Many of his acquaintances volunteered to be hypnotized simply out of curiosity, but others hoped for relief from troubling ailments like insomnia, asthma, excessive smoking and recurring headaches.

Bernstein's success rate continued to be remarkably high; he found himself amazed at how easily he could induce trances, implant post-hypnotic suggestions, and relieve his friends' pains and discomforts. He had developed an impressive ability in a very short time. He began to wonder just how far he could go with it. How skilled could he eventually become?

His fascination with age-regression hypnosis increased. He knew that other hypnotists had guided their subjects back to earlier points in their lives, enabling them to relive forgotten or repressed memories. Was he capable of doing that, too?

One of Morey Bernstein's best subjects was Virginia Tighe, a young Pueblo housewife who was able to go easily into very deep trances. During one session, Bernstein had taken Tighe back through her childhood memories to her days in kindergarten. Tighe accurately described her favorite doll, her best dress and her little dog, Buster.

Fascinated, Bernstein took her even further back — to infancy, to the time in her life when the only word in her vocabulary was "wa-wa" for "water." After this session, the captivated hypnotist wondered just how far back this remarkably receptive woman could really go? Was there any possibility at all that her mind held memories of a life lived prior to her present one?

Bernstein had read a great deal about reincarnation, but he was highly skeptical of the entire concept. It seemed like a lot of nonsense to him. But then, so had the concept of hypnosis.

On the night of November 29, 1952, the Bernsteins invited the Tighes to their home. After Virginia stretched out comfortably on the davenport, Morey asked her, as he had many times before, to give her total concentration to a lighted candle he held a few inches from her eyes. Within minutes, she entered a very deep trance. With the reels of Morey's tape recorder turning, one of the most remarkable hypnotic sessions of all times began.

First Bernstein led Virginia Tighe back again through her earliest years, from age five, back to four and then to one. "Now," the hypnotist urged, "go still farther back. I want you to keep on going back and back and back in your mind until you find yourself in some other scene, in some other place, in some other time."

Virginia Tighe was silent for several moments. Then she began to speak in a child's voice with a heavy Irish accent. She told how she had scratched the paint off her bed by digging her fingernails into every bed-post. She had done it, she said, because she was angry. Afterward, she noted sadly, she "got a terrible spanking."

Bernstein was almost breathless as he asked, "What is your name?"

"Bridey," the child's voice replied.

"Your name is Friday?"

"No," said the child, a bit impatiently. "Bridey. I'm Bridey Murphy."

Bernstein and the others present in the room that night had just heard, for the first time, a name which would soon become famous nationwide, a 156-year-old name that would lead to an international search for her identity.

As calmly as possible, the stunned hypnotist asked, "Where do you live, Bridey?"

"Cork," replied the little girl within Virginia Tighe. "It's in Ireland." Under Bernstein's continued question-ing, she went on to tell of her family (a mother, father and a brother), her home (a white, wooden house) and her school (Mrs. Strayne's Day School where she learned "house things and proper things"). She was eight years old, and the year was 1806.

"Now see yourself when you're a little older," Bernstein urged.

Bridey Murphy, in her thick Irish brogue, began telling the story of her life —or more accurately, her lives.

She had grown up in Cork, married a Catholic barrister named Brian MacCarthy after which they moved to Belfast. Although she had been raised as a Protestant, Bridey attended St. Theresa's church with her husband. She and Brian became close friends of the church priest, a "Father John." Bridey bore no children during her lifetime, but she remained largely content with her simple, pleasant life. At the age of 66, she took a tumble down a flight of stairs and died shortly thereafter.

"What happened after your death?" the spellbound Bernstein asked. "Did you watch them bury you?"

"Yes," Bridey answered. "I watched them ditch my body."

She went on to say that after her burial, she returned to her home where she spent her time "just watching." She could see Brian and her friends, but she couldn't talk to them. She felt no pain nor did she need to eat or sleep. Eventually, Father John died. Although she wasn't sure when since "time doesn't mean anything." He came to visit her and they talked "just like we always did."

Bridey felt that her life in the spirit world was merely a transitory period, a time of waiting. Then, in 1923 in Iowa, she "became born again" as Virginia Tighe.

Shaking with excitement, Morey calmed himself before gently asking Virginia to clear her mind and return to the present time and place. She awoke from her trance and Morey shut off the tape recorder. Everyone in the room sat in benumbed silence. Something momentous had just happened, something far beyond anyone's ability to comprehend. But as incredible as this hypnotic session had been, the ones that followed proved even more amazing.

In the second session, Bernstein asked Tighe if she could see herself before she lived as Bridey Murphy. "Uh-huh," the Irish voice replied. "Just a baby...little baby... dying." Bridey remembered very little about this brief life; she knew neither her name nor the year during which she died as an infant. She could go no farther back than that.

Bernstein took her back again to the time she lived in Ireland. Carefully, he questioned her on the details of her day-to-day life. He encouraged her to talk about seemingly trivial things, such as, "What did you eat for breakfast?"

"Muffins mostly," the child answered. "Eat muffins n'jam n'milk n' fruit."

The enthralled hypnotist cautiously pressed her for names and addresses for anything that could be substantiated later. He learned that in Cork she had lived in a neighborhood called The Meadows. Bridey could not remember her address in Belfast, but her home was 20 minutes walking distance from St. Theresa's church.

Bridey didn't travel much in that lifetime, so her memories of what few journeys she made were fairly vivid. She remembered her trip with Brian when they moved to Belfast. She could recall the names of the villages along the route and the rivers and lakes as well. Bernstein quizzed her on the Irish customs and traditions of her time. Bridey recited the prayer she always said before meals, and she talked about a tiny cup called a "brate" from which people drank before making a wish. When asked if she danced, she replied, "Uh-huh. As little girls go, I was a good dancer. I remember dancing, dancing by myself."

"Did you have a favorite dance?" she was asked.

"I liked the Morning Jig," she said.

Bernstein carefully controlled his excitement as he said, "I want you to go through the Morning Jig in your mind. Remember all the little steps. Watch yourself dancing. After you awaken tonight, you will be asked to do that jig, and you will do it very easily. I won't talk to you for a few minutes. Rest and relax. Think about the Morning Jig."

Several minutes lapsed before Bernstein awakened Tighe. He waited a few minutes more, to allow her drowsiness to pass. Bernstein then suggested she go to the center of the room and do the jig for the witnesses who were present.

Tighe looked utterly bewildered; she seemed to have absolutely no idea what Bernstein meant. But she went to the middle of the hushed room anyway and began to concentrate. Suddenly, her expression brightened; her body became dynamic, her feet began to fly. The Colorado housewife whirled about in a swift, nimble Irish dance which ended in a graceful jump and the placing of her hand to her mouth.

Very quickly, before Bridey Murphy's expression faded from Virginia Tighe's face, Bernstein asked, "Why did you put your hand on your mouth?"

"That's for a yawn," Bridey answered. Then Bridey was gone and a dazed Virginia sat back down on the couch. The remarkable session had ended —in a dance that greeted the morning sun with a joyous leap and a sleepy yawn.

Three more hypnotic sessions were held in the coming weeks, each revealing more and more minute detail about Bridey's life. The time had now come for Bernstein to begin checking out the details, to seek their verification. By studying atlases, he soon discovered many of the towns, rivers and lakes that Bridey mentioned did exist. With the help of a friend, Sam "Stormy" MacIntosh, he delved into all the literature available in Pueblo's libraries. He was able to substantiate several more bits of information Bridey had given.

Bridey had named "Sorrows of Deirdre" as one of her favorite books; she admitted being enthralled by the legend of the Irish folk-hero Cuchulain and said she sometimes read the Belfast *News-Letter.* Research by Bernstein and MacIntosh, cursory at this point, confirmed that during Bridey's lifetime (1798-1864), the book, the legend and the newspaper were quite popular.

Very little more than that could be checked out in a town the size of Pueblo back then, but as luck would have it, Bernstein was scheduled to make a business trip to New York. While there, he allowed himself time to do as much researching as possible. He was pleased, if not surprised, to find Bridey's memories of Old Erin were quite accurate.

Bernstein's curiosity about the many unfamiliar words in Bridey's vocabulary led to some fascinating discoveries. She had referred to a surgeon as a "chirurgen," which turned out to be the archaic form of that word. The wishing cup which in Bridey's heavy brogue sounded like "brate" was spelled "quate." Once, she called a coarse man whom she disliked a "tup;" *Roget's Thesaurus* lists "tup" as a synonym for male, similar to "chap" or "rounder."

To Bernstein, the most intriguing word Bridey used was "ditched" in reference to her burial. It took quite a bit of page-turning to learn that during the Great Irish famine of 1845-47, there actually were mass burials in ditches. The term "ditched," although not in current Irish usage, was a colloquialism at that time.

Many other words from Bridey, such as "barrister" for lawyer, or "linen" for handkerchief, or the exclamation "Oh, Mother Socks!" when she was exasperated, were words Virginia Tighe never used, but an Irish woman of Bridey's time definitely would have uttered.

The search for some of the places Bridey named

proved more difficult. One place in particular, Baylings Crossing, seemed impossible to find. Calls to the Irish consulate, the British Information Service and the British and Irish Railways netted only one firm fact: Baylings Crossing did not appear on any Irish maps. Yet Bridey Murphy distinctly remembered being there.

It seemed Bernstein had hit a dead-end on that reference until one weekend he talked to a woman who had lived in Northern Ireland during World War II. When he asked her if she had ever heard of Baylings Crossing, the woman replied, "Oh my, yes. I bicycled through it many times. I'm not surprised you couldn't find it on a map. It's such a tiny place, it simply wouldn't *be* on a map."

Once again Bridey had been vindicated.

Bernstein left New York convinced he had established enough facts to go public with this incredible story. He wrote a book which included complete transcripts of all five tape recordings and all of his other findings. The book, published in January 1956, had the title, "The Search for Bridey Murphy." Instantly it became the nation's Number One bestseller. More than 170,000 copies were sold before March that year, and 30,000 record albums of the tapes were sold during that same time. Bridey-mania swept the country.

"Bridey Murphy Puts Nation In A Hypnotizzy," blared *Life* magazine. In a five-page article, *Life* described "a craze both giddy and serious" that had put a "considerable part of the U.S. under an Irish spell, and the spell is becoming deeper and wider as fast as the written word, awed gossip and the televised image can spread it."

Hypnotic sessions became a popular fad comparable to the Ouija board and seance spirit-searches of the 1920s and 1930s. Hypnotists, both sincere and fraudulent, exploited the Bridey phenomenon in night-clubs, theaters and family parlors. Everyone, it seemed, was suddenly eager to experience or at least witness age-regression hypnosis. Bridey Murphy costume parties were in full swing nationwide. Guests were asked to "come as you were," so many women came dressed as Bridey herself in antique, lacy dresses and old-fashioned hats. Most partygoers, however, preferred to think they had been Cleopatra, Napoleon or Arab sheiks in their previous lives.

Two popular songs, *The Ballad of Bridey Murphy* and *The Love of Bridey Murphy*, appeared on records. Perry Como's new release, *Did Anyone Ever Tell You, Mrs. Murphy?* rose on the Hit Parade charts even though it had nothing to do with the now-famous little lady from Belfast.

In cocktail lounges, a new drink was being served: Reincarnation Cocktails. Consisting of vodka, maraschino liqueur, lemon juice and a topping of flaming rum, the drink was guaranteed to make anyone imbibing it wish for a new life the next morning. Stand-up comedians told Bridey Murphy jokes: "Did you hear about the guy who read Bridey Murphy and changed his will? He left everything to himself."

Not everything about the furor over reincarnation was light-hearted. In Shawnee, Oklahoma during February 1956, a teenaged boy named Richard Swink wrote a note: "...I am curious about the Bridey Murphy story so I am going to investigate it in person." He then shot and killed himself with a rifle.

Bernstein was astonished by the tumult he had caused. True, he had been forewarned. His friend Stormy MacIntosh had bluntly told him, "When your book is published, Morey, you will be dubbed a crackpot, a fanatic, or a lunatic. You'll be getting phone calls and letters from mediums, cultists and faddists. To top it all, there will be those who are offended in the mistaken impression that you are challenging their religious beliefs."

Morey Bernstein had braced himself for that kind of reaction, but there was no way he could have anticipated the magnitude of the mania he unleashed.

Virginia Tighe, too, was startled and disturbed by the overwhelming response to the book. It had been difficult enough for her to listen to the tapes after the trances, to hear a foreign voice coming unbidden from within herself. But after the initial shock, she calmly accepted the possibility that she might actually have lived other lives. Her only concern was to get on with her current life.

When Bernstein had started the book, she had asked him to conceal her true identity. The hypnotist readily agreed and called Virginia Tighe "Ruth Simmons" throughout the text. This well-intentioned but naive attempt to shield Tighe from the glare of the national spotlight protected her privacy for only a short time. The search for Bridey Murphy very quickly turned into a search for Ruth Simmons, and in a small city like Pueblo, it didn't take long for out-of-town journalists to discovered who she really was.

Just as she dreaded, Tighe was besieged by reporters. She steadfastly refused to talk to them or to grant interviews, and she emphatically turned down a $1,000-a-week offer for nightclub appearances in Denver.

The *Denver Post*, whose reporters were among those turned away from Virginia Tighe's door, decided to take a different approach to this sensational story. The newspaper sent an investigative journalist, William J. Barker, to Ireland to conduct an intensive, in-depth hunt for "Bridey evidence." Barker returned to Denver three weeks later, dazzled by the corroborative facts he had uncovered.

The reporter's diligent search through Irish historical archives, old maps and city directories enabled him to prove that many of the most obscure places Bridey talked about actually had existed. She had said she grew up in a residential area adjoining the city of Cork, a pastoral suburb she called The Meadows. A beautifully drawn map of Cork dated 1801 showed an identical neighborhood known as Mardike Meadows.

As he traced Bridey's honeymoon journey on the maps of the old coach road from Cork to Belfast, Barker located another crossing, Doby, that Bridey had mentioned, but which was no longer on any contemporary maps. Bridey had also told of shopping in Farr's and John Carrigan's stores in Belfast; Barker found both stores listed in an old city directory.

By the end of his stay in Ireland, Barker had gathered enough information to enable him to write an 18,000-word article for the *Denver Post's* Sunday supplement. The case for Bridey Murphy's having been a real person now seemed very strong. Then, the debunkers went to work on the story.

A lot of people, especially deeply religious persons, could not accept the possibility of reincarnation. To them, the concept was an assault on established religious doctrines. The story of Bridey Murphy had to be firmly and decisively refuted. Among the most adamant of these fundamentalists was the Reverend Wally White of the Chicago Gospel Tabernacle.

Early one bright spring morning in 1956, Reverend White came knocking on the door of Virginia Tighe. Bible in hand, he introduced himself as the current pastor of the church where she had attended Sunday school after her family had moved to Chicago in 1927. "I have not come to write about you," he assured her. "I only want to pray for you."

Suspicious but curious, Virginia Tighe allowed Reverend White to come inside. As soon as he was admitted, however, the minister bombarded her with polite but persistent questions about her childhood in Chicago. Where had she lived? Who were her friends and neighbors there? Did her family pray before meals? Had she liked to dance as a child?

She tolerated the intrusive preacher only briefly before sending him on his way. It was not until sometime later that she learned the true purpose of his visit. Wally White was assisting an investigative team from the Hearst tabloid, the *Chicago American*, in preparation for an expose of the Bridey Murphy phenomenon.

Using information White provided as a starting point, reporters for the *Chicago American* began interviewing people who had known Virginia Tighe as a child. When the series was published in June 1956, the newspaper contended that Tighe's memories under hypnosis were "merely a recollection of her youthful days in this lifetime."

The tabloid revealed Virginia had an aunt, Marie Burns, who was "as Irish as the lakes of Kilkenny and had regaled the young girl with tales of Ireland." An even more interesting disclosure was that an Irish immigrant named Bridie (not Bridey) Corkell lived for a time across the street from Virginia's childhood home. And, the newspaper said, Bridie Corkell's maiden name had been Murphy.

The newspaper went on to report that young Virginia had lived less than two blocks from a city park ...a "meadow" where she must have played many times. According to the articles, she had taken elocu-

tion and dancing lessons and had become quite talent-
ed in reciting "lengthy Irish dialect routines" and in
"dancing jigs for pennies on the streets of Chicago."

Soon after the Chicago articles, *Life* magazine ran
another feature with the headline "Bridey Search Ends
At Last. She was in Chicago all the time."

Bernstein and Barker were startled and embar-
rassed by the articles, as was the *Denver Post*. The
Post's editors sent its own feature writer, Bob Byers, to
Chicago to double-check the allegations published in
the *Chicago American* reports. It did not take Byers
long to discover that the tabloid's expose was as full of
holes as an Irish potato field.

Byers was a perfect choice for investigator. He
did not believe in reincarnation, but he did believe in
honest, objective and factual journalism. To Byers,
there was nothing more disgraceful than twisting facts
to fit them into a preconceived premise. His talk with
Marie Burns proved to him right away that this was
just what the *American's* reporters had done.

Virginia's Aunt Marie was of Scottish-Irish
descent, all right, but she had been born in New York,
not Ireland, and had spent most of her life in Chicago.
She could not have "regaled" her niece with tales of Ireland because she had no such tales to tell.

The *American* had been equally sloppy, or perhaps deliberately deceptive, in its references to Bridie
Murphy Corkell. While it was true that Corkell grew up
in Ireland and did live for a few years across the street
from Virginia's Chicago home, she had never lived in
either Cork or Belfast. Corkell spent her Irish childhood in County Mayo in the extreme midwestern part
of Ireland. In her trances, Virginia Tighe spoke only of
Cork in extreme southern Ireland and Belfast, a north-
eastern Irish city. Not once did she mention anything

about County Mayo. Why, Byers wondered, did Tighe possess such a wealth of detailed and uncannily accurate information about two cities so distant from the place where Corkell lived?

Byers also noticed that the time frame didn't fit. Bridie Corkell was born in 1897, 33 years after Bridey Murphy claimed to have died, and 99 years after her birth. If the Irish stories Tighe related under hypnosis were recollections of tales spun by Bridie Corkell, why did they all concern events that occurred in an earlier century rather than in Corkell's own time?

While Byers gathered information in Chicago, William Barker set up an interview with Virginia Tighe in Pueblo. Since her own integrity was now at stake, she at last agreed to talk to a trustworthy reporter. She told Barker she remembered her Aunt Marie quite well, but had never once heard her speak of Ireland; it was, after all, a country that Marie Burns had never visited. Tighe's memories of her neighbor, Bridie Murphy Corkell, were somewhat vague. "I've thought about it a lot, as you can imagine," Tighe told Barker. "Mrs. Corkell had several children whom I knew, but I have no recollection of ever having talked to Mrs. Corkell herself. I don't remember ever hearing her first name, and I certainly had no way of knowing her maiden name."

Regarding the nearby "Meadows," Tighe acknowledged there was a lake-front park near her home. "But," she said with a laugh, "can you imagine any Chicago kid calling a city park 'The Meadows?' I certainly wouldn't have."

Barker then asked about the claim that she once had the ability to recite Irish dialect routines. "The only part of that implication that sounds remotely right is that I did take elocution lessons in 1935 or 1936," she responded. "I can't remember anything specifically about what I was taught, but my teacher, Mrs. Saulnier, was very strict about the correct usage of the English language. She never taught her pupils dialects."

Anticipating Barker's next question, Virginia Tighe went on to say, "The accusation that I danced jigs in the streets for pennies is ridiculous. My parents would never have allowed that! As for those Irish jigs I'm supposed to have learned, they were called the 'Charleston' and the 'Black Bottom.'"

The two reporters uncovered enough discrepancies in the *Chicago American's* expose for Byers to write a rebuttal which the *Denver Post* carried on its June 17 front page under the headline, "Chicago Newspaper Charges Unproven." Barker wrote two additional chapters for the next edition of Bernstein's book.

Many of those who believed in the Bridey phenomenon took this new information as confirmation of the long deceased Irish woman's existence, but others had by now dismissed the whole episode as a strange release of Virginia Tighe's subconscious memories; others concluded the whole thing was an elaborate hoax perpetrated by Bernstein and Tighe.

Perhaps the strongest argument against the hoax theory is the fact that both Bernstein and Tighe turned down offers of more than a quarter of a million dollars for public appearances. True, Bernstein did receive some rather handsome royalties for his book and the sale of his recordings, but Tighe steadfastly refused the hypnotist's offer of a share in the royalties. One must consider Virginia Tighe's own feelings about her mystifying experience. As she told William Barker, "The thing that makes all this so difficult is that I'm not ready to say whether I do or do not believe in reincarnation. My husband and I have tried to keep open minds. We only wish they'd let us keep the record straight as well."

Morey Bernstein, who had once been a disbeliever himself, was left wondering what he's stumbled onto. Had he, as he phrased it in his book, taken "the first step on the long bridge" into the unknown? He continued to read about reincarnation and found that many, many others, including Rudyard Kipling, Plato, Voltaire and even Benjamin Franklin, had believed in the concept.

Bernstein was particularly fond of a verse written by a 19th century poet, John Masefield:

> *I hold that when a person dies,*
> *His soul returns again to earth.*
> *Arrayed in some new flesh-disguise:*
> *Another mother gives him birth.*
> *With sturdier limbs and brighter brain*
> *The old soul takes the road again.*

Bibliography - Chapter 2

Barker, William J. "The Truth About Bridey Murphy." Denver Post supplement. March 11, 1956.

Bernstein, Morey. **The Search for Bridey Murphy.** Garden City, New York. Doubleday & Company, Inc. 1956.

Boar, Roger and Blundell, Nigel. **Mystery, Intrigue and the Supernatural.** New York. Dorset Press. 1991.

Brean, Herbert. *Life* magazine. Chicago. Time Inc. March 19, 1956 and June 25, 1956.

Sheehan, Peter and Perry, Campbell W. **Methodologies of Hypnosis.** Hillsdale, New Jersey. Lawrence Erlbaum Associates. 1976.

3

HAUNTED PLACES
& GHOSTLY TRACES

Colorful Colorado, home to cougars, bears and elk, is also natural habitat for ghosts. Any of its long abandoned cabins, forgotten cemeteries, rustic hotels, Nineteenth Century mansions and its craggy peaks and caves seem quite capable of hosting supernatural beings.

It is hard not to feel the presence of a long-vanished homesteaders or mountain men when you hike past the shell of an abandoned high country cabin. It is a reflex action to see a spectral figure standing momentarily in the hallway of one of Colorado's old Victorian hotels. Can anyone walk past a gold rush mansion, glance up at a window and not expect to see a ghostly hand closing the faded lace curtains?

Colorado ghosts are as varied as the places they haunt. Some can be both seen and heard, while others are visible but silent. A few are mere presences which enjoy borrowing a living person's body once in a while.

Earl Murray, a western author who investigates paranormal phenomenon, once wrote about a curious experience related to him by Don Coldsmith of Emporia, Kansas. In December 1983, Coldsmith had gone to visit his daughter and son-in-law who run a ranch in the Brown's Park area of northwestern Colorado. One brisk morning, Coldsmith accompanied his son-in-law in his pickup as he checked the winter cattle pastures.

While they bounded along the rough trails, the young rancher pointed out some of the local landmarks. "See that old cabin way out there, Don?" he gestured. "Everyone calls that 'Butch's Cabin.' They say it used to be a hideout for Butch Cassidy and the Wild Bunch."

Don Coldsmith was immediately intrigued. He knew historic accounts verified that the Wild Bunch did, indeed, maintain a cabin hideaway in Brown's Park shortly after Butch was released from prison in 1896.

One of the Wild Bunch, Matt Warner, had described it in his memoir, *Last of the Bandit Riders*: "As I fixed it up, and stocked it with horses, it became more and more the headquarters of my old outlaw and half-outlaw pals... Cassidy come to live with me and my cabin was crowded every night by a drinking, poker-playing, bragging crowd."

Coldsmith wanted to visit this mythic site, so later in the day, he borrowed the pickup and drove back to look at the cabin. The dilapidated building was tucked away on a low knoll above a broad meadow, a perfect place for an outlaw's hideout. Anyone approaching the cabin could be seen from a considerable distance.

Coldsmith crossed the meadow and peered in the cabin door. The old hut was, of course, in pretty sorry shape. The roof had collapsed long ago, and the rotten log walls were falling apart. Coldsmith leaned against the door frame and placed his other hand on the opposite side of the door.

What happened next was something he would always find difficult to describe. It was a sudden realization that someone from the past had entered his body.

He had become a different person; someone else was now controlling his body's movements. He found himself turning in the doorway to face the meadow. Involuntarily, his head moved slowly back and forth as his eyes scanned the edges of the grassy expanse. He felt incredibly alert. His vision seemed keener. In the distance, he saw an antelope he had not noticed earlier, stepping lightly through the afternoon shadows.

Once his eyes, which were no longer his own, identified this moving object, Coldsmith felt the presence within him relax. For several minutes more, the spirit seemed to simply enjoy the sight of the alpine vista stretching out in front of the cabin. Then, as quickly as it had come, the spirit invader departed, leaving Coldsmith standing in the sagging doorway in a state of breathless wonderment.

Had the ghost of a long-dead outlaw risen within

him and used his living eyes to watch a scene it remembered but could no longer see? Don Coldsmith left the crumbling cabin in Brown's Park believing that was exactly what had happened.

The spirit population of Colorado's haunted cabins must surely number into the thousands. Although many of the oldest log or adobe homes have collapsed and disintegrated, spirits often still linger at those sites, startling modern day visitors. The ghost of Shipman Park cabin is a typical example.

This cabin was built in 1876 by two men remembered as Shipman and Green. It was located somewhere high in the Medicine Bow range in what is now the Roosevelt National Forest. The two young men had chosen this remote spot to set up a base camp for a fur trapping venture.

During the summer, they chopped down lodgepole pines and cleared a small area upon which they erected a sturdy, one-room log cabin with a rock fireplace. Then they headed back to town to fill backpacks with supplies for their new home: flour, beans, and blankets especially. By the time the first snowflakes began to fall, they were securely settled in for the winter.

Or so they thought.

The winter of 1876-77 was one of the worst on record. Blizzard after blizzard blasted the Medicine Bow Mountains. Shipman and Green were rarely able to tend their trap lines or hunt the fresh meat they had counted on. Then one night, Shipman grew seriously ill. He complained of a severe, nearly unbearable pain near his stomach.

Green knew there was nothing he himself could do for his friend; he would have to go for help. The nearest ranch, the Forrester place, was at least 12 miles away. But since it was all downhill, Green knew he could make it there in a single day.

He dragged a log into the cabin and positioned it on the dirt floor so that one end was in the fireplace and the other was within reach of Shipman's bed. "This should keep you warm till I get back," he said as he strapped on his snowshoes. "Just keep pushin' it in as it burns. I'm goin' down to see the Forresters. I'll bet they'll have some medicine or somethin' that'll fix you right up, partner."

Green plunged off into the deep, loose snow, switch-backing his way down from the sub-zero mountains to the Forrester's foothills ranch. The old couple were just lighting their evening lantern when he thumped his mittened fist on their door. "Mister'n Missus Forrester! I need your help real bad," he blurted out. "My partner is terrible sick. He's got a fever that's burnin' him up and a pain in his guts that's near killin' him."

The Forresters glanced at one another and frowned. It sounded like appendicitis to them. If it was, the snow-bound young man was likely doomed.

Mrs. Forrester rummaged through her cupboards. "We don't have much, Mister Green," she said over her shoulder. "But perhaps we can ease that poor boy's pain. Here's a bottle of mint oil which will soothe his stomach, and I'll make up some poultices that will help some."

Mr. Forrester promised to return to the icy cabin the next morning. "If we take turns breakin' trail, we should get to your cabin before dark."

With the earliest light, the two men set forth into the bitter cold, trudging as fast as possible through the deep snow. Their efforts were all in vain. Shipman was dead when they reached him.

Forrester and Green cleared away the snow alongside the cabin and chipped out a shallow grave. They buried Shipman in his blankets and marked his resting place with a buffalo skull and a ring of stones.

"Shippy was the best partner a man ever had," Green mourned. "I just wish we'd thought to bring along a Bible, so we could've read a few words for him. Well, tomorrow, I'm goin' to pack up and head out of here. Ain't no point in stayin' on now."

After Green packed up and left, the lonely cabin remained vacant for more than 20 years. Its timbers sagged and rotted and part of the roof collapsed. In the broad valley below, several additional ranches had been established between 1890 and the turn of the century. These new ranchers often rode past the aged cabin while searching for strays or cutting corral poles. Sometimes they took refuge within its decaying walls during particularly rough weather. It was those infrequent visits that lead to the eerie stories.

A rancher named Frank Farmer was the first to report having seen a ghost at Shipman's cabin. He and one of his hired hands had holed up there during a snow storm in the winter of 1890. Just before dark, a mysterious figure walked past the doorway, paused, glanced in, and quickly faded into the falling snow. Farmer had quickly jumped to his feet and peered out the door. No one was there, nor were there any footprints.

Before long, other cowboys began telling similar tales. On snowy days, just at dusk, a pale phantom was often sighted moving about in the dimming light.

Jim Hardman, a Medicine Bow cattleman, may have been the last one to see the apparition. He said he had ridden past the cabin during the winter of 1909. It was just a pile of decomposing logs by then, and the chimney had fallen on top of the hearth. Still, through the softly falling snow, Hardman saw a solitary figure standing beside the ruins. When he shouted out a greeting, the figure vanished.

One of Colorado's most poignant ghost stories concerns a spirit which visits the old Buckskin Joe cemetery near the little town of Alma. The tale begins in 1861 when a lovely young woman (whose real name is forgotten but whose stage name was "Silverheels") toured Colorado's opera houses and theatrical halls. She had a popular song-and-dance routine that had her high-stepping in silver-heeled shoes.

After she gave performances in Fairplay, she traveled over to the bustling mining camp called Buckskin Joe. There, she danced and sang for the utterly enthralled miners.

In the Buckskin Joe camp, where the ratio of men to women was 70 to one, any woman was a welcome sight, but Silverheels was unlike any woman the miners had ever seen. She was exquisitely beautiful, her voice was angelic and she danced like a dream.

After a few evenings, she prepared to continue her tour at the next mining town. But her admirers in Buckskin Joe begged her to stay and lavished her with gifts. Silverheels agreed to stay on in Buckskin Joe for a few more nights. According to legend, she left the camp before dawn so she wouldn't have to say goodbye to the men who adored her.

The miners never saw Silverheels again, but they never forgot her. One day, about a year later, word came to the lonely mining camp that Silverheels was dead. Historic accounts differ, but the cause of death was reported as either pneumonia or small pox. The most romantic version was that one of the towns she visited was stricken with a small pox epidemic; she stayed on to care for the sick, contracted the disease herself and died.

In any event, the miners of Buckskin Joe were shocked and grief-stricken. They held a memorial service for her and named the mountain above the camp "Mount Silverheels." That name still appears on topographic maps of the area today.

As time went by, many of the miners themselves died; by accident, illness or the deadly cold.

In 1870, a cemetery was laid out on a piney ridge not far from the camp's cluster of tall, wooden buildings. Today, it is one of the more enchanting, off-the-beaten-path sites in Colorado. The graves are scattered almost randomly among the pines and aspens. Deer can often be seen strolling from tombstone to tombstone through the mottled sunlight. All is quiet and peaceful in Buckskin Joe cemetery.

After the mines played out in 1872, the mining camp became a frontier memory. But the people of the tiny mountain hamlet of Alma still continue to bury their deceased loved ones in this idyllic little graveyard. The townsfolk made frequent visits to the cemetery to place bouquets of wildflowers on the graves and to stand in the tranquil silence to reminisce.

Over the years, those who went to the Buckskin Joe cemetery to remember departed loved ones grew convinced that the graveyard is the stage for an apparition. Some people reported that at twilight, they had seen a beautiful, young woman in a long, white dress moving among the tombstones and wooden crosses as the last rays of sunlight radiated from her auburn hair. Others, those who had been here at night, swore they heard a sweet, ghostly voice singing in the darkness. They all knew who it was, of course... Silverheels returns from time to time to serenade the long-dead miners who had once been her greatest admirers.

Two of Colorado's most unique ghosts are sisters. Both were the daughters of a mystic woman who insisted on being called "Madam Crawford." She was a spiritualist who claimed to be able to speak to the dead during seances. She had gotten her education in Leipzig, Germany, and was an accomplished classical pianist when she immigrated with her two children to America in the late 1880s.

Why she left her husband is uncertain, but her quest for a place where she could focus her spiritual energies became obvious when she moved from Boston to Manitou, Colorado in 1891. At that time, Manitou hosted a small but dynamic community of spiritualists whom Crawford was eager to join. Her second reason for choosing the small Colorado town was even more important. Manitou, known now as Manitou Springs, was a famous health resort and Madam Crawford hoped its highly-touted mineral waters would help her youngest daughter, Emma, recover from tuberculosis.

Emma Crawford was a delicately beautiful young woman. A faded photograph of her shows a frail, yet curiously determined individual. Her dark, lovely eyes give a hint of sorrow. It almost seems that she already knew her destiny.

Not long after the Crawfords arrived in Manitou, Emma met a handsome young man named Brent Hildebrand. He was a construction engineer for the Manitou-Pike's Peak Cog Road, a project which when completed would be the highest railroad in the world. They fell in love and planned to marry after the rail link was finished and Emma had recovered from her illness.

Brent was away from Manitou much of the time, working high on the slopes of Pike's Peak. Emma spent most of her days sitting on the sunny porch of the Crawford's two-story frame house on Capital Avenue. Like her mother, Emma Crawford must have been psychic, for one spring night just before she went to bed, she told her mother that the spirit of an Indian man had appeared before her in the darkness. He had said he would return soon to guide her to a sacred spot near the summit of nearby Red Mountain.

Two days later, when Madam Crawford stepped out onto the porch, she was startled to find Emma's rocking chair empty. She grew increasingly alarmed as the day went by and there was still no sign of her ailing daughter. At last Emma came walking out of the twilight. Her usually pale face was flushed with excitement; her eyes were wide with wonder.

"I did it, Momma!" she exclaimed breathlessly. "I followed the spirit all the way to the very top of Red Mountain. And I tied my scarf to a piñon tree to prove I'd truly been there."

Emma Crawford was almost totally exhausted. She went immediately to bed. Her mother and older sister, Alice, sat beside her throughout the long night, listening to her struggle to breathe. Just at dawn, she opened her eyes for the last time. She took her mother's hand and said, "Tell Brent I want to be buried at the foot of the tree where I tied my scarf." Her head fell back on the pillow, lifeless.

Word of Emma's death was quickly sent to Brent Hildebrand. He hurried back to Manitou. Told of his fiancee's dying words, he vowed, "If that's what Emma wanted, that's how it will be."

In the morning, twelve pallbearers in dark somber suits worked in shifts to carry Emma's coffin up the rugged slope of Red Mountain. Her grave, near the scraggly piñon tree, was ready, so as the late after-

EMMA CRAWFORD. Perhaps she knew she was destined to live in the spirit world.

noon shadows stretched out over it, the pallbearers lowered Emma into the ground. While shovels full of rock and gravel thudded on the coffin, Brent untied Emma's scarf from the tree, folded it carefully and tucked it into his coat pocket. Alone, ahead of the others, he walked down from the darkening mountain.

History does not reveal where Brent Hildebrand went after that, but neither he, nor Madam Crawford nor the remaining daughter stayed much longer in Manitou.

The Crawford's spiritualist friends made frequent trips to Emma's grave to hold seances. Upon their return, they always reported having seen and communicated with the dead girl. They said they learned that the Indian spirit, knowing Emma was about to die, had come to show her a sacred place where she could rest her psychic soul.

Most Manitouans dismissed the spiritualists' stories; after all, those were the kinds of tales spiritualists were expected to tell. But a little more than a year after Emma's death, two of the Crawford's former neighbors, Mrs. and Mrs. W.S. Crosby, visited the grave. They came back down from Red Mountain and confirmed the spiritualists' tales.

"Me and my missus ain't never believed in ghosts," Crosby said. "But we both seen little Emma up there. She looked kinda misty, but it was her all right."

During the next fifteen years, dozens of hikers told of sighting the pale apparition; a few even claimed to have seen the ghost of an Indian man standing nearby. A good many Manitouans came to accept the fact that they had a haunted mountain on the outskirts of town, but none of them had any way of knowing that another ghost was soon to take up residence in their little community.

In 1908 Alice Crawford Snow returned to Manitou. She had been living in Los Angeles with her mother following a brief, but turbulent marriage. Life had not treated her well during those difficult years. Marriage to a prominent attorney had ended in divorce and her attempt at an acting career resulted in humiliating failure. Alice was a bitter and despondent woman when she came back to Colorado.

Perhaps the depth of her despair was expressed by her choice of a home; she rented the loneliest house in Manitou, the Iron Mountain Castle. This somber, bleak, stone mansion stood on a barren hill a full mile from the edge of town. Though its chimney and its sharply-peaked tower were tall, the castle always seemed to give the impression that it was squatting and brooding on the landscape.

Alice Crawford Snow grew very reclusive and seldom left the castle. Then one cold winter night, she wrote a suicide note, left it on her bed table and shot herself with a revolver.

Iron Mountain Castle remained empty for more than a year after Alice's death. Indeed, it has been vacant throughout most of its long history, primarily because it cost a fortune to heat, and its entrance road was nearly impassable in winter. A family named Davis moved into the mansion in 1910. They soon found that, in addition to the problems of staying warm and clearing the driveway of snow, they had another problem to deal with. Alice was still there.

When Alice's ghost first made her presence known, it was in a subtle way. The Davis' heard faint music, as if someone was playing an old phonograph somewhere in the house. They searched for the source of the music, but because it was so soft, they could never quite tell where it was coming from. Although it was a puzzling sound, it was not unpleasant and the Davis children were not frightened by it.

Then the furniture started moving around.

Chairs and tables levitated off the floor and drifted from one room to another. Closed doors were found open in the morning, and open doors slammed shut with a bang during the night. The Davis' never actually saw Alice Crawford's apparition, but all too frequently, they did see a white, glowing light in the corner of a hallway at the top of the stairs.

The Davis family concluded that moving to Iron Mountain Castle had not been a wise decision. Within a year or two after they departed, Louis Hakes and his wife bought the mansion and settled into its chilly gloom. They repeatedly experienced the same phenomenon. By the time the Hakes fled from the castle it had a well deserved reputation as a haunted house.

As might be expected, the spooky old mansion attracted Manitou's school children by the scores on Halloween. Its blank windows stared down like baleful eyes at the shivering youngsters who gathered in the shadows to nervously savor their fear.

Rufus Porter, a lifetime Manitou resident, always chuckled when he looked back at those deliciously scary childhood nights. "We stood talkin' in low voices and occasionally, one of us would part from the group and walk around the corner of the haunted building. But from there on, he or she ran as fast as possible around the old castle, skidded to a stop at the front and sauntered leisurely back to the group to dare another of us to 'walk' around the castle. It had to be alone, one kid at a time, and some of the kids were too scared to even try it."

As spooky as Iron Mountain Castle was in those days, it was destined to become even more arcane within a few more years. Its mystery deepened in 1924 when a seemingly unrelated event occurred on the summit of Red Mountain.

The summer of 1924 was one of unusually heavy rains. One particular downpour caused a landslide which swept the grave of Emma Crawford down the slope and into the trees below. A couple of young boys hiking through the debris found some bones and a fragment of a skull, along with a casket handle and a brass plate with Emma's name on it. These meager remains were reinterred in Manitou's Crystal Park Cemetery in a grave appropriately lined with piñon pine boughs.

Emma was now forever gone from the sacred spot to which she had been led by the Indian spirit. Her displaced spirit must have drifted about in search of a new resting place. It seems only natural that she might move in with Alice's spirit in Iron Mountain Castle.

The old mansion was unrented at the time, and it remained vacant until the following June when a newly wed Manitou businessman carried his bride across the castle's threshold. The young couple had, of course, heard stories about the old building, so they were well aware that they might be sharing it with a ghost. But they had not counted on living with two ghosts.

Proof that Alice's sister had also taken up residence in Iron Mountain Castle was not long in coming. The honeymooners had spent no more than a week in the mansion before they were awakened late one night by the faint sound of piano music. Although they searched the house nervously, they could never find the source of the music. Emma Crawford, unlike her sister, had taken piano lessons from Madam Crawford, and played it rather well. Apparently she still did, even though there was no piano in the castle.

Most of Colorado's ghosts prefer lonely, out-of-the-way places where they are seen or heard by a limited number of people. One exception to this general rule is a ghost who is said to haunt an old hotel in Empire. This particular spirit is probably Colorado's most controversial.

This ghost story begins, as most do, following a tragic event. Shortly after the end of the Civil War, a Union Army veteran named William Ludley Peck traveled west with his wife and their little daughter, Millie. Peck staked out several mining claims in the Empire area and made a fairly substantial sum of money. He used it to build a fine, two-story hotel where he and his family lived on the upper floor.

When Millie Peck was only five years old, her mother died of tuberculosis. The young girl never accepted her parent's death; she was sure her mother was somewhere in the hotel, and spent a good deal of time searching for her.

Late one afternoon or early evening, when the hallways were darkening and before the lamps had been lit, Millie Peck stumbled and fell down the hardwood staircase. She was unconscious when she was carried back up to her room, where she died in her bed.

After this tragedy, William Peck sold the hotel and returned to the East. New owners of the hotel quickly discovered they had an unusual, and permanent guest. Frequently their paying guests, especially those who slept in Millie's room, came downstairs in the morning to complain that their rest had been severely disturbed.

Women told of being awakened by a child's voice speaking directly in their ears, asking "Mommie?" Oth-

THE PECK HOUSE. Does a delicate ghost really whisper in the ears of sleeping guests?

Photograph by Jack Kutz

ers told of hearing rustling sounds in the closet; they found the clothes they had hung up were rearranged during the night. Stranger still, some swore they heard a child skipping through the hallway past their rooms. On one chilling occasion, several people burst out of their rooms because they distinctly heard someone tumbling down the stairs. Of course, no one was there when they looked.

However, Millie *has* been seen numerous times. Once, a woman became hysterical when she looked down the stairs and saw the crumpled body of a little girl lying at the bottom. When she screamed, the ghostly figure faded away.

The maids who worked in the hotel claimed to have seen Millie frequently. Sometimes they would step out of a room and see her standing in the hall. She would smile and disappear.

The Peck House changed hands a few more times over the years, but it has always been maintained in its original Victorian style. Grainy old photographs of the Peck family still hang on the walls of the small, antique-filled parlor. The steep stairway leads up to the narrow, white-washed hallways on the second floor. The old hotel has all the ambience and old-style comfort of a bygone era. It also still has its ghostly reputation.

The people who ran the hotel prior to the present owners took the ghost quite seriously and tried to verify its existence. They held seances in the hotel, with inconclusive results. The psychics they invited to inspect the premises said they did feel a definite presence as well as "cold spots" in various places. Earl Murray, after visiting the Peck House, said the presence of a spirit was "very strong" in Millie's room, especially around the bed.

But the current owners absolutely do not believe their hotel is haunted. They insist that other people who have sensed Millie "brought her ghost with them in their minds and when they left, they took her ghost away again." The owners further point out that if a ghost does exist, they themselves would surely have seen it by now.

How, then, does one account for the sightings that have been reported over a period of more than one hundred years, mostly by people who did *not* expect to see a ghost?

One possibility is that the ghost of little Millie Peck can only be perceived by people who are psychic, knowingly or not. Maybe her spirit is so subtle, so ethereal, that only rare individuals can be touched by it.

How to Visit Colorado's Haunted Places

To reach the Peck House, take Interstate 70 from Idaho Springs for 12 miles to the State Highway 40 exit. Two miles later, you will be in Empire. Keep an eye out for a large "Peck House Hotel" sign on the right side of the road. The hotel is a short way uphill behind this sign. It is a pleasant place to stay; if you are resolutely convinced there are no such things as ghosts, you can expect a peaceful night's sleep. On the other hand, a stay at the old hotel might offer an unforgettable encounter with little Millie.

To visit Buckskin Joe cemetery, drive northwest from Fairplay on State Highway 9 for eight miles to Alma. Watch for the intersection where the post office and the fire station face each other across the street. Turn left past the tiny fire house onto the graveled Park County Road 8. Go 1.4 miles to Alma's town reservoir. One-tenth of a mile beyond the reservoir, the "Hoosier Autotour" sign marks the turnoff to the cemetery. A mere four-tenths of an uphill mile farther, the little road will have taken you into the serenity of this rustic graveyard. The most likely place to see or hear Silverheels is in the oldest part of the cemetery where the wrought iron and wooden grave enclosures stand.

Bibliography - Chapter 3

Crosby, W.S. *Frontier Times* magazine. Austin, Texas. Western Publications. June-July, 1965

Daniels, Bettie Marie and McConnel, Virginia. **The Springs of Manitou.** Denver. Sage Books. 1964.

Martin, Maryjoy. *True West* magazine. Austin, Texas. Western Publications. January, 1985.

Murray, Earl. **Ghosts of the Old West**. New York. Dorset Press. 1988.

Porter, Rufus L. *Frontier Times* magazine. Austin, Texas. Western Publications. October-November, 1979.

Smith, Fay Emory. *Frontier Times* magazine. Austin, Texas. Western Publications. April-May, 1965.

4

The Orneriest Little
Ghost in Denver

Haunted houses are, for obvious reasons, not exactly the most desirable places to live. Most people do not enjoy being awakened in the middle of the night by strange noises, unexplainable lights or footsteps on the stairs.

A few folks, however, have lived quite comfortably with ghosts. They have not only accepted their spectral co-tenants, but have grown very fond of them. These tolerant people are fascinated, rather than frightened, by the spirits. They forgive their capricious behavior and finally come to regard the ghosts as special members of the family. Two such people were former Denverites, Robert and Dorothy Bradley.

The Bradleys were both obstetricians who moved to Denver in 1962. They developed an immediate love for the city and began searching at once for just the right house. Without much difficulty, they found it in May of that year. It was a large, many-roomed Tudor-style mansion in a prestigious residential neighborhood.

Built in 1917, this grand old house looked both proud and friendly. Beneath its blue shale roof tiles, ivy climbed its stone walls; its spacious lawn was bowered by great trees. Dorothy Bomar Bradley took one look at the place and told her husband, "We'll take it." She also very quickly came up with a name for their new home. By combining the first part of her husband's last name with the second part of her maiden name, she christened the mansion, "Bradmar."

From the outside, Bradmar did appear deserving of an elegant name. The manor's interior, however, was badly neglected and in need of considerably repair. The Bradleys hired an interior designer named Karl Vogel to plan and supervise the restoration. As the three of them walked through the empty rooms assessing the work that would have to be done, Vogel casually asked, "Has anyone told you about the house's reputation?"

When the Bradleys shook their heads, Vogel said, "Well, the last person to live here was a little, old widow lady named Ethel Work. It seems that shortly before her death, she told her servants, friends and family members that when she died, she wanted to lie in state in front of the fire place —right here, in the drawing room— and on that night, she would split the ceiling beam above her casket. Sure enough that's exactly what happened.

"I've always been pretty skeptical of ghost stories, but as you can see, the beam *is* split, cracked lengthwise, starting near the center. But it's still structurally sound, so you needn't worry about it. There are much more important things that we need to fix up."

In the following days, Vogel diligently busied himself drawing up plans to modernize the house without altering its historical character. One evening, he glanced at his watch and realized he had worked later than he'd expected to. Rather than drive all the way to his home only to return in the morning, he decided to spend the night in Bradmar on a cot in an upper room. He had no more than settled into his blankets when he heard the locked front door open and close.

Vogel listened intently as footsteps echoed lightly across the emptiness of the lower floor. Moments later, the back door opened and closed. Vogel dashed to a window overlooking the backyard. No one was there.

When the Bradleys arrived the next day, Vogel asked whether they had come into the house the previous night. They both replied "no," so the puzzled designer explained, "Well, someone did. Someone who didn't need a key." With a trace of a smile on his face, he gazed at the cracked beam above his head. "If you two don't mind, I think I'd like to stay in Bradmar again tonight. It might prove to be an interesting evening."

Later, as the old house darkened, Karl Vogel sat on the edge of his cot, waiting and listening. This time, he was not particularly surprised to hear the door he had securely locked creak open and swing shut. As the footsteps clicked lightly on the floor, Vogel hastened to the top of the staircase and spoke to the darkness below. "Mrs. Work," he said firmly. "'If you don't like the way I'm restoring your house, why don't you come up here and tell me about it?"

The footsteps stopped abruptly. Vogel tightened his grip on the banister, bracing himself for the appearance of a phantom. Instead, whoever was downstairs stamped off to the back door, opened it and slammed it with an emphatic bang. Vogel was both disappointed and relieved. As he told the Bradleys in the morning, "I'm not really sure how I would have reacted if the old girl had actually come up the stairs."

Strange things continued to happen at Bradmar as the repair work progressed. An electrician was hired to completely rewire the house, but he became utterly frustrated because the lights kept turning on and off by themselves. Often he would find that wires he had carefully connected had been mysteriously disconnected. On one occasion, when he was standing on a ladder, he felt himself being shoved. He landed on the floor.

Despite these annoyances, the restoration was finished by the end of the summer. The Bradleys were eagerly, though apprehensively, anticipating their long-awaited move into the house. They had taken up temporary residence in the home of a close friend, Siegwalt Palleske, a professor of foreign languages at the local university. On the last night of their stay in Palleske's home, they all settled down to watch television in the living room.

Dorothy Bradley was totally absorbed in the program until, out of the corner of her eye, she noticed the large philodendron hanging from the ceiling was waving a single leaf at her. She was staring at it in disbelief when a sound which she later described as a "thunderous bolt of noise" shook the entire house. Since the bang seemed to have come from within the house rather than outside, everyone jumped up and searched each room.

They found nothing out of order and no explanation for the stunning boom. But as soon as they went back to the living room, a soundless "brilliant blinding light" flashed before their eyes. Siegwalt Palleske lit a cigaret with trembling fingers. "What is *your* ghost doing in *my* house?" he asked his friends.

"Maybe she know we're moving in tomorrow," the shaken Robert Bradley suggested. "I'd say this was either a welcome or a warning."

Perhaps surprisingly, the transfer of the Bradleys belongings into Ethel Work's former home went smoothly the next day. Nothing disturbing happened. Before nightfall, everything had been carried inside and the Bradleys spent a peaceful, uninterrupted night within the stone walls of Bradmar.

Morning came and Robert got up early. Taking special care not to awaken his still sleeping wife, he went quietly down the stairs to the drawing room. This was a moment he had looked forward to for a long time; he was about to enjoy his first morning cigar in Bradmar.

He unwrapped a panatela and reached for the heavily-weighted lighter standing on a marble-topped table. But the lighter rose, floated out of reach and dropped on the carpet with a soft thud. Undoubtedly, the cigar also dropped from the doctor's mouth. When he bent down to pick up the lighter, it rolled away from him.

Bradley chuckled out loud. To the empty room, he said, "Well, Mrs. Work, I think you've made your point. Quite obviously, you don't want me smoking in your drawing room. Very well, from now on, I will confine my smoking to my den."

Later, at breakfast, Robert told Dorothy about the incident but added, "I think we can live with her. In fact, we might even grow to like her."

Ethel Work continued to make her presence known in a variety of ways. One of her most persistent habits was turning on lights at unexpected times. She repeatedly switched on the light on the headboard of the Bradleys' bed while they slept, flipped on the lights in the hallways and sometimes, when they were reading in the drawing room, she clicked the three-way light bulbs in the lamps from the first position to the third.

Once, while Robert lay on the couch reading, the window shade rolled up to give him better light. On another occasion, Dorothy, who was seated in the kitchen, nearly spilled her coffee when an invisible force struck a Venetian blind hard enough to set it swinging wildly. Dorothy had planned to bake bread that morning, so she found herself wondering if this was Mrs. Work's way of telling her to quit dawdling and get busy with the baking.

At times, the ghost caused noises for no apparent reason other than to announce she was there. The sounds ranged from a single clear note on the cello standing in the corner to an extremely unpleasant gong-like clang from out of nowhere. Whenever the Bradleys entertained guests, Ethel was quite likely to tap on the ceiling or the walls a time or two, particularly when she was the topic of conversation. She also took an impish delight in throwing water on Dorothy's legs when she least expected it.

One of the mischievous spirit's oddest pranks was so peculiar that neither Dorothy nor Robert could do more than speculate about the motivation. One morning, while Dorothy was home alone, she glanced out the library window and saw a dead fish lying on the window sill. She bent down and, with her eyes just inches away from the glass, peered at it closely. Its glistening scales reflected a variety of colors and markings unlike anything she had ever seen before. She ran out of the house and around to the window, but when she got there, the fish was gone.

The incident left her completely perplexed. Why did Ethel make a fish appear and then disappear? Could she have been trying to show Dorothy that, as a spirit, she could travel to faraway places and bring things back? Or was it just a ditsy old ghost's idea of a joke?

Some of Ethel Work's stunts proved to be much more than just attention-getting, poltergeist pranks. The Bradleys soon learned that their rascally supernatural housemate possessed a very impressive precognitive talent which enabled her to foresee future events. She attempted to warn the Bradleys of impending serious problems.

The first display of this remarkable capability came on a Sunday afternoon in the winter of 1962. The Bradleys' grandchildren had come by for a visit, so they, too, witnessed this exceptional manifestation.

As the children walked with their grandparents through Bradmar's great hall, the large brass chandelier hanging above them began to jump up and down on its long, heavy chain like a bobber on a fishing line. The children stood transfixed, mouths hanging open.

"Oh dear, Ethel's really upset about something. I wonder what's wrong?" Dorothy said.

She found out two hours later when a phone call told the Bradleys that a family member had just been hospitalized for a severe illness. Though the relative made a good recovery, the family experienced considerable stress and worry during the next few days.

Of course, an incident of this sort —a poltergeist phenomenon occurring at the same time that a family member took sick— could be dismissed as coincidence if it happened only once. But at Bradmar, the astonishing occurrence of psychic activity preceding an illness or an injury to a relative or close friend happened time and time again.

In the spring of 1963, every light in the house turned on at exactly 4:30 a.m. for three consecutive mornings. On the fourth day, one of the grandchildren became ill. A few months thereafter, a cousin and her small baby came to visit the Bradleys. That night, a light beside the infant's bed came on; in less than 24 hours, the baby became so seriously ill that several hospitalizations and surgery were necessary. Approximately one year later, a bedroom light went on in the daytime just before Siegwalt Palleske's elderly father injured himself when he fell in his backyard.

Most of Ethel Work's psychokinetic performances took place within "her" home, but it soon became evident she was by no means a stay-at-home ghost. She clearly enjoyed getting out once in a while to accompany Dorothy on her busy rounds. On two occasions, once on the street and once in a Mexican restaurant, she playfully tossed water on Dorothy's feet, apparently just to let her friend know she was there.

Dorothy Bradley was at that time very active in a local little theater group. She spent many evenings in rehearsals. One night, just as the cast prepared to leave the theater, one of the stage props, a rocking chair, began to creak rhthymically back and forth as if an invisible critic was giving approval to the play's progress. Several times after the group locked the doors and headed for their cars, they glanced back from the parking lot to see the upstairs lights shining brightly down at them.

Needless to say, Dorothy Bradley was always the one who had to go back inside and shut them off again.

At a dress rehearsal, Dorothy readied her make-up kit and assembled her costume changes. She sorted through her collection of artificial jewelry which she used only for plays. Her part called for her to wear a wedding band and an engagement ring. But when she looked for the imitation diamond ring she always wore, the wedding band was missing.

She searched everywhere, through all her purses and dresser drawers, but she could not find the ring.

Knowing she could easily get a replacement before opening night, she proceeded to take the rest of her costume jewelry to the theater. Upon opening the jewelry box in her dressing room, she discovered to her amazement that the wedding ring was back again, lying beside the engagement ring.

By now, Dorothy was somewhat accustomed to this sort of event, so she felt more pleased than surprised. She wore the rings through the run of the play, taking them off each night and leaving them in her dressing room. On the last night of the play, when she left the stage, she looked at her hand and saw that only the engagement ring was on her finger. The wedding band was gone.

She was totally baffled. The ring could not have fallen off since the engagement ring was above it. Besides, it was a very tight-fitting ring. Still, it had vanished and she never saw it again.

The amazing phenomena the Bradleys constantly experienced led them to an intensive study of the supernatural. They read all the available literature on the subject and became active members in the Spiritual Frontiers Fellowship, a national organization composed of people from all walks of life who have had similar encounters with the paranormal. At the fellowship's annual conventions in Chicago, the Bradleys met many other "sane and solid citizens," as Dorothy described them, who also had family ghosts in their homes.

In Denver, both Robert and Dorothy became in much demand as lecturers on spirit manifestations. "Spirit communication is not limited by the known senses of sight, hearing, touch, smell and taste," they used to tell their audiences. "The 'passed-over' entity often expresses regret that his or her loved ones, still obstructed by earthly life, cannot as yet share the beauty offered by their heightened senses with their far broader spectrum of perception."

The Bradleys continued to live in Bradmar until 1980 when, at last, they sold the mansion and moved away. The current owners shun publicity; they do not welcome either curious visitors or sightseers. But chances are about dusk this very day, they will say, "Hello, Ethel. How are you this evening?"

Bibliography - Chapter 4

Bradley, Dorothy Bomar, and Bradley, Robert A. **Psychic Phenomena: Revelations and Experiences.** West Nyack, New York. Parker Publishing Company, Inc. 1967.

Kelley, Brenard. *The Denver Post* Sunday Supplement, *Contemporary Magazine*. Denver Post, Inc. October 28, 1962.

Myers, Arthur. **The Ghostly Register: Haunted Dwellings, Active Spirits. A Journey to America's Strangest Landmarks.** Chicago. Contemporary Books, Inc. 1986.

5

Alferd Packer's
Ghastly Ordeal

Charles Adams, Indian agent for Los Piños Ute Reservation, stood at the window of the agency's mess hall, gazing out as he finished the last of his breakfast coffee. It was a spring morning, April 15, 1874, but beyond the window it still looked like winter. Snow was still deep in the high country; it was bitter cold, and the sun, vaguely visible through the ground-level clouds, would not warm anyone that day.

The winter had been long and hard. The Utes, as always, had accepted it, hunkered down and survived. But Adams knew there were other people out there in that snowbound wilderness who were not as wise, resourceful or stoic as the Indians. What had happened to all those greenhorns from Back East and those adventurers from the warm Deep South? What had become of all those impetuous men from gentler climes who had passed through his territory last fall on their way deep into the mountains, unwilling to wait for fair weather to begin the quest for gold, silver and furs?

Adams was about to turn away from the window when he caught a glimpse of movement in the cold whiteness that veiled his lonely outpost. He wiped the steamed-over glass pane with the palm of his hand and leaned forward for a better look.

A dark figure was emerging from the frigid mists, lurching and stumbling through the snow. The man's feet were wrapped in pieces of blanket. He was limping badly. His long, black hair was matted and tangled above a bearded face crusted with ice formed by his labored breathing.

Adams thumped down his coffee cup and hurried to the door. He swung it open just as the gaunt figure raised a hand to pound on it. The hollow-cheeked face confronting the Indian agent was cadaverous. At first, the man did not speak. Then his voice came from within him like an echo from a tomb. "They left me to die," he said as he staggered into the mess hall.

The Indian agent caught him under the arms and eased him into a chair near the pot-bellied stove. He shouted toward the kitchen, "Bring this man something hot to drink!" The cook was already hastening out with a cup of coffee. "Warm up some soup," Adams barked. "And bring a pail of warm water." He began stripping away the frozen pieces of blanket beneath which were a pair of bare feet, cold as ice.

A bucket of steamy water was delivered and after the anguished man had soaked his feet, a little life seemed to return to his sunken, grey eyes. "Don't try to talk now," Adams advised. "Drink some of this broth. Get some sleep. Later on you can tell us what happened."

The skinny, wild-haired man eagerly gulped down the soup and allowed himself to be led to a bunk where he was covered with warm, woolen blankets. By evening, he had recovered enough to begin telling the story of his ordeal.

"My name," he said, "is Alferd Packer."

He extended his thin, trembling hand and Charles Adams clasped it gently. Little did Adams know he had just shaken hands with a man whose name was destined to become one of the most infamous in Colorado history.

Packer was 32 years old. He had grown up in a Pennsylvania Quaker family, but he had joined the U.S. Army at the age of 20. Within a few months, he was discharged for medical reason; he suffered from severe epilepsy. Rejected by both the army and his pacifist parents, he became a wanderer, drifting farther and farther west, working at whatever jobs he could find. In 1873, he wound up in Salt Lake City, completely down on his luck, nearly destitute and ready to accept any employment available to him.

As he trudged through the streets, he learned that two entrepreneurial men, Robert McGrew and George Tracy, were putting together a small prospecting team to head into the Colorado gold fields. Packer applied for a job at once.

"We can use another teamster," McGrew acknowledged. "Me and George are having trouble finding men willing to head into the mountains this late in the season. It's risky, I know, but we want to get a headstart on all the others who'll be following us in the spring. If you're willing to take that risk with us, I'll give you a job. I can't promise you a share in anything we find in Colorado, but I will pay you fair wages."

"Done," said Alferd Packer. "I'm ready to go whenever you are, Mister McGrew."

On November 17, 1873, McGrew, Tracy and 21 men rolled out of Salt Lake City with wagons carrying ample provisions and weapons. After the first two weeks of travel, Packer began having frequent seizures at night. The other men, who had never seen an epileptic before, were frightened and repulsed by Packer's convulsions, but McGrew pitied him and cared for him as best he could until each frenzied seizure had passed.

The wagon train ran into its first real problem when it crossed the wild Green River in southeastern Utah. Here, two wagons overturned in the swift current. Their precious cargos swirled away. The wintery weather slowed the party's progress much more than McGrew and Tracy expected. By the time the expedition entered Colorado, everyone was starting to worry.

One snowy morning, the men looked up from their smoldering campfires to see a group of Indians silhouetted against the greyness on the ridgeline. When the Indians began riding slowly down toward the wagons, everyone picked up a rifle or unholstered a pistol. One Indian rode boldly ahead of the others, his long braids bouncing lightly on his blanketed chest.

"I am Ouray the Arrow, chief of the Uncompahgre Utes," he said in perfect English when he halted his horse in front of McGrew.

The expedition leader breathed a sigh of relief; he had heard of this legendary Ute leader. "Lower your rifles," he told the men behind him. "These are not hostiles."

Chief Ouray was widely recognized as a wise and pragmatic man, highly respected for his efforts to maintain the uneasy peace between his people and the white invaders. Eventually Ouray and all members of the seven Ute nations would be driven from their mountain homelands, but in 1873, the land McGrew's party was crossing still belonged to the Indians.

"We wish only to pass through your reservation," McGrew told Ouray. "We are heading for the San Juan Mountains."

"Your passage will be a perilous one," the Indian replied. "This is a cruel land in winter. It would be best if you came with us to our camp. There we can give you shelter and sell you food."

The wagon train followed Ouray and his warriors south along the rough, snow-drifted trail paralleling the Gunnison River. At last they reached a secluded valley where the Utes had set up their winter camp.

"You are welcome to stay with us and wait for better weather," Ouray offered.

McGrew shook his head. "I appreciate your offer, chief, but me and Tracy didn't come all this way to stop now. We'll rest a couple of days, buy some food and push on."

He turned to the other members of his party to ask, "How about the rest of you? Are you still with us?"

The shivering men hesitated. They were chilled to the bone and the warm glow in the teepees looked very inviting. "If you choose to winter here, we can pay you no wages," McGrew warned. "Those of you with the guts to go on will be paid in full, come spring."

Sixteen of the 21 men decided to remain in Ouray's camp. On February 1, 1874, McGrew, Tracy and three others set off for the tiny, distant settlement of Saguache. Alferd Packer was among those who stayed behind, but he was not at all sure he had made the right decision. He was safe and warm for the time being, but he was also out of a job again.

Five of the others who had quit the expedition also were having second thoughts by the time they had warmed up a bit. True, they could survive the winter comfortably in Ouray's camp, but then what? "I think we oughta head outta here and catch up with Mister McGrew," Packer told them. "If he lays over a few days in Saguache, we could get there in time to rejoin him."

The other five men agreed. Although none of them owned a horse or possessed frontier experience, each shouldered up a pack loaded with food for seven days and on February 5 they plunged off into the snow.

The six men had little in common. In addition to Packer, there was a Californian named George Noon, a pair of former Pennsylvania farmers, James Humphreys and Isreal Swan, a German immigrant, Frank "Reddy" Miller, and a taciturn, moody fellow known as Shannon Wilson Bell. Fate had thrown this motley crew together; it lured them step by step into a frozen hell where their worst possible nightmares were about to come true.

When they left Ouray's camp, the Ute chief urged them to follow the Gunnison River, because if they tried to take a short cut through the mountains, they would surely become lost. But within a few days, the hapless trekkers came to the cold realization that if they stayed on this longer route, they would run out of food long before they reached the Cochetopa Pass trail to Saguache. They had hoped to supplement their supplies by shooting an occasional deer, but so far they had sighted no wild game.

Turning desperate, they decided to disregard the chief's advice and headed off cross-country.

It was a terrible mistake.

The snow in the long mountain valley they chose for their passage was so deep they could not plow through it. They clamored up onto the barren ridge line to face a shrieking wind which lashed them furiously as they plodded along.

On the morning of their eighth day, six very frightened men divided the last cup of flour. They dipped it out of their last cotton sack and tried to swallow it before the fierce wind snatched it from their numb fingers. Throughout the next day, they found only a few dried rose hips and some pine gum to eat. Most of the men were now praying constantly as they stumbled on.

Late that afternoon, Packer sighted an alpine lake in a valley below the ridgeline. The men staggered down to it and walked out onto the snow-covered ice. With hatchets, they chopped holes and crouched above like Eskimos hoping in vain to spear a trout with sharpened sticks. It was a futile effort; they caught no fish but did manage to claw out a few snails from the frozen shoreline mud.

That night, they camped in the trees and used the last of their matches to build a campfire. When morning came, they scooped up a coffee pot full of glowing embers and trudged on with their precious fire. At nightfall, they huddled in a makeshift pine-bough shelter and ate their leather footwear.

As the men's strength faded, their pace grew slower. Even so, Packer was having trouble keeping up with the others; his feet, wrapped like everyone else's in strips of blanket, were causing him excruciating pain. He limped badly.

Adams listened intently as Packer told his story. "I was slowin' everybody down, so one morning, they just went off and left me. Somehow, I kept on goin'. I don't know how I done it, 'cause there's a whole lot I don't even remember, but I finally saw the chimney smoke from this agency, and I praised God and came on it. What day is this?"

"April 15," said Charles Adams.

Alferd Packer passed a shaky hand across his forehead. "Good Lord" was all he could say.

On April 16, Preston Nutter, one of the ten men who wintered in Ouray's camp, came riding into Los Piños. He and Packer stared at each other in surprise. "Preston!" Packer exclaimed. "I never thought I'd see you again."

"Where are the others?" Nutter asked. Packer retold his story. Nutter listened without comment until he had finished. Then he pointed at the knife hanging from Packer's belt. "That's Reddy Miller's knife, isn't it? I'd recognize that fancy handle anywhere."

"Yes, it is," Packer nodded. "Miller stuck it in a tree the night before they left me, and he went off and forgot it."

Later in the day, when Nutter was able to talk alone with Adams, he said, "There's something wrong with Alferd's story. I don't think he's tellin' us the whole truth. If Miller stuck that knife in a tree, how's come Alferd's also got the sheath? Besides, it's damned hard to believe those men would just go off and leave him."

"It is hard to accept," Adams agreed, "but under those dreadful circumstances it is quite possible."

Packer stayed on at the agency outpost until the

spring melt was under way. The trails became less hazardous, so Alferd Packer set off once again for Saguache. The tiny mountain hamlet was at that time little more than a cluster of cabins scattered around a saloon, a general store and a boarding house. Saguache offered no opportunities for employment, but Packer convinced the storekeeper to allow him to sleep in the back room in exchange for chopping firewood and doing chores. Packer also expressed a willingness to pay for his own groceries.

"He don't spend much," the grocer confided to the saloonkeeper. "But I got a feelin' he's got more money than he lets on about. There's somethin' fishy about that fella."

The local constable, a tough, steely-eyed man named Lauter, was also growing suspicious of Alferd Packer. "None of your companions ever made it to Saguache," the lawman told him. "I gotta find out what happened to them. I'm organizing a search party, and you're going to guide us back to the place where you last saw them."

"I don't *never* want to go back to those mountains," Packer shuddered.

"I didn't say you had a choice," Lauter replied. "We're leavin' first thing in the mornin'."

Shortly after sun up, Lauter, Packer and three newly deputized Saguache citizens rode off for Los Piños. From there, accompanied by Agent Adams, they followed Packer as he tried to retrace his route. Within a few miles, Packer seemed to become confused and bewildered. "I can't remember. Nothin' looks the same without the snow. I may have come in over those ridges ahead of us, or through those mountains off that way. I just don't know."

"You're lyin' to me, Alferd," Lauter said bluntly.

"And I know why you're lyin'. You killed those men, didn't you? Killed them and robbed them. Well, Alferd Packer, I'm placing you under arrest for murder and after I find the bodies of your victims, you're gonna hang."

Lauter took Packer back to Saguache where he was locked in the log cabin that served as the village jail. With a large posse, he combed the mountains searching for the missing men. He found nothing.

One day in early June, a group of writers and artists from *Harper's Weekly* arrived in that part of Colorado on assignment to sketch, paint and describe the beautiful Colorado Rockies for the magazine's eastern readers. They rode forth from Gunnison in a fancy, rented buggy, south along Lake Fork through the idyllic alpine landscape. At noon they stopped, hopped out of their carriage and trooped merrily up the hillside to a grove of trees where they planned to picnic amid the wildflowers.

Five minutes later, they came streaming back down the slope, retching and gagging and holding their hands over their mouths. They scrambled into the buggy, slapped the reins and churned the wheels all the way back to the nearest farm.

"Why," they asked the surprised farmer, "are all those dead men lying up there on that hilltop beyond this valley?"

The *Harper's* entourage had stumbled onto the five bodies Lauter searched for. It had been a very gruesome sight. One of the artists, John Randolph, later made a sketch of the scene from memory, showing how the corpses were sprawled on the ground with large portions of flesh cut from their legs, arms and ribs. Some of the limbs were bare of flesh clean to the bone; two of the ribcages were completely stripped.

ALFERD PACKER. Convicted of murder and cannibal-
ism in what is considered Colorado's most heinous
crime, he was a man no one knew how to pity.

The farmer, Mezekiah Musgrave, led Lauter's posse to the site a few days later. After the bodies were examined, they were buried on the spot and Lauter headed back to confront Packer.

"You'll be interested to know we found the bodies," the constable told his nervous prisoner. "And, you'll probably be even more interested to know that there's a whole bunch of men down at the saloon right now talkin' about takin' you outta this jail and stringin' you up. At this point, I ain't sure I want to risk my life protectin' yours. So it's time you made a confession. I want the truth. All of it."

"It was Bell that done it," Alferd Packer swore. "And then, I killed him. He was actin' pretty crazy toward the last. Talkin' to himself all the time. Had a real wild look in his eyes.

"I went off to find dry firewood late in the afternoon, and I took along one of the rifles in case I saw any game. Because of the condition of my feet, I was movin' real slow, so it was after dark when I got back to our camp," Packer said quickly, as if finally eager to unburden his conscience. Then he paused a bit, staring off beyond the cabin wall.

"Bell had a big campfire goin' and the first thing I saw was Reddy Miller lyin' face down in the snow. Swan, Noon and Humphreys was wrapped in their blankets inside our windbreak, and Shannon Bell was kneelin' by the fire, roastin' a big piece of meat.

"He looked up at me, the firelight blazed in his eyes, and he seized his hatchet and rushed on me. I dropped to my knees to escape the blow, pulled the trigger of my rifle and killed him with a single shot that went sideways through his body.

"I expected the other three would arouse at the sound of the shot, but no one under the blankets stirred. I crawled over to them and I could tell by the blood-stained snow that they were all dead. Their skulls had been crushed as they slept."

Alferd Packer spread his thin, spider-like fingers over his face, making it difficult for Lauter to hear the next few words. "It seemed like I was in a dream," he mumbled. "I felt no sense of horror. No fear. No loneliness. I just felt kinda serene and very drowsy. I crawled into my blankets and fell asleep.

"When I awoke, I rekindled the fire and finished roastin' that piece of Reddy Miller's leg. I ate it, but it come right back up. So, I sliced off a slab of Shannon Bell's leg, cooked it and ate it real slow. I ate like that for several days. Little by little, my strength revived enough so I could push on.

"I put some raw flesh in a sack, took Reddy Miller's knife and all the money from the dead men's pockets. I know it wasn't right to rob the bodies, but somehow, it seemed to give me hope. It kept me goin' because I knew that if I didn't give up, I would spend that money on food, on crackers and tins of sardines, cheese and bread.

"I don't know how many days I waded through the snow before I sighted the agency, but when I knew I was safe at last, I threw away the meat sack. I went on in and lied to Mister Adams about what happened.

"I don't know what will be my fate now, but I do feel thankful that I will no longer have to tell lies."

Lauter stared silently at this pathetic man for a long time. Finally he said, "I can't pass judgement on you, Alferd. Only God can do that. But, I give you my word, you ain't gonna get lynched as long as you're in my custody."

The constable left Packer's log-walled cell, locked the door and strode down to the saloon. He pushed his way through the drunken crowd of angry men to demand their attention.

"Alferd Packer has given me a confession. He's gonna be dealt with justly." He placed his hand on his pistol. "All of you are goin' home now, and you're gonna take your damned rope with you."

The mob dispersed as did the threat of a lynching.

In the morning, Lauter accompanied the cook from the boarding house as she carried Packer's breakfast to the jail. As they approached the cabin, they saw the door was slightly open. The prisoner was gone.

Years later, Packer would say he had help in making his escape. Someone — he never said who— felt sorry for him, believed he killed Shannon Bell in self-defense and forgave him for eating human flesh and robbing the dead. That someone probably knew that he would have committed the same deeds under those nightmarish circumstances.

Many citizens in Saguache suspected Constable Lauter of freeing his own prisoner. After all, Lauter was the one with the easiest access to the jail key. Could it be that this tough, old lawman had a soft spot in his seemingly callous heart? No one will ever know.

Alferd Packer disappeared for nine years. He, like so many others in that tumultuous era, changed his name and ran from his past.

In 1883, Frenchy Cabezon, one of the 21 members of the original 1873 expedition, arrived in Wagonmound, Wyoming. Cabezon had become a peddler who traveled from town to town in a wagon clattering with pots and pans. As he was tying his horses to a hitching rail, he glanced up and saw Alferd Packer coming out of a store. Cabezon ran at once to the sheriff's office. Within minutes, Packer was wearing handcuffs.

The fugitive was taken by rail to Denver where

scores of people showed up at the depot for a glimpse of the infamous "Colorado Cannibal." From there he was escorted under heavy guard to Lake City to stand trial in the Hinsdale County courthouse.

Now Packer changed his story again. The murders, he told the judge and jury, did not occur all at once. When he came back to camp with his armload of firewood, he found four of the men engaged in cutting up the body of Isreal Swan. Quickly, Swan's choicest parts were roasted and devoured by all five of the emaciated, half-mad, half-dead men.

He said Reddy Miller was the next one to be sacrificed. A few days after Swan's death, as Miller bent down to pick up a stick of firewood, Bell sprang out of the snow and smashed his skill with a hatchet. Humphreys and Noon were soon dispatched in the same swift, cruel way. Now Packer faced Bell alone.

He said he tried to guard himself at all times, but with the snow falling so heavily, he couldn't always tell where Bell was lurking. He knew this predatory fellow cannibal was stalking him, circling the edge of the campsite with his blankets clutched around his shoulders like a cape, waiting for just the right moment to pounce.

When that moment came, Alferd Packer was ready.

"He rushed me swinging his rifle," Packer testified. "I parried the blow, and the rifle was broken by striking a tree. I then hit Bell with a hatchet until he was dead. I no longer had any fear of death except by starvation. I cut up the body of my companion, ate as much as I could, and packed away considerable for future use, and then I resumed my tramp, the sole survivor of a party of six."

The jury did not accept Packer's story. They

quickly found him guilty of all five murders. Judge M.B. Gerry sentenced him to be hanged. Packer was locked in an impregnable iron cage, an escape-proof lattice work of flat, heavy bars with a small, rectangular opening at the bottom of the door through which food could be pushed in and a bedpan could be pushed out.

In the days immediately following the trial, many writers and reporters sat in front of that stark, black cage and interviewed the "Man-Eating Maniac." Invariably, they came away with sharply contrasting impressions of the man to whom they had just spoken. Author Alice Polk Hill wrote: "He has large grey eyes, cold yet nervous. He paces like one sneaking away or creeping upon a victim. Anyone possessing even a moderate knowledge of human nature would say he belonged naturally to the criminal class."

Conversely, a reporter from the *Lake City Silver World* observed: "I confess I did not see a 'fiendish look' or discover 'nature's mark of a murderer, beast or ghoul' which the enterprising reporters of the Denver press tell us he carries on his face. On the contrary, he has a pleasant face and mild grey eyes. He is, in fact, a rather mild-looking and mild-mannered person."

Meanwhile, the local sawmill was cutting the planks for the gallows scaffold. The Hinsdale County sheriff, Clair Smith, was passing out special, much-coveted invitations to the execution. Packer's attorneys, A.J. Miller and Aaron Heims, hastily filed an appeal on a legal technicality. They pointed out that the territorial criminal codes had been repealed when Colorado became a state in 1876, and the new state laws contained no provisions allowing death sentences for murders which took place prior to statehood. Four days before Packer was scheduled to drop through the scaffold floor, a stay of execution was announced. Now Packer became a resident at the Gunnison jail while his lawyers sought a new trial. It is said he passed his time weaving "hair trinkets" to sell to the many visitors who came to stare at him.

The second trial of Alferd Packer was finally held in August of 1886; he had waited three years to hear himself declared guilty again. Judge William Harrison sentenced the now totally despised cannibal to serve 40 years — eight years for each victim— in the state penitentiary at Canon City.

Annually, Packer applied for a gubernatorial pardon. Annually his request was turned down. In 1900, a *Denver Post* columnist, Mrs. Leonel Ross O'Bryan, who wrote under the byline "Polly Pry," championed Packer's cause. In her columns, she emphasized that Packer's guilt had never been proven beyond all reasonable doubt. Backed by many readers who agreed with her, O'Bryan personally pressured Colorado Governor Charles S. Thomas into granting Packer a full pardon on January 10, 1901.

In his letter of thanks to Mrs. O'Bryan, Packer wrote: "Oh, God, if I could have died in the mountains, I would have been spared 28 years of misery. I have never closed my eyes in sleep since without that ghastly vision of the smoldering campfire, the dead companions and the lofty pines drooping with their weight of snow, as if keeping a sorrowful death-watch. But, those who have never been without their three meals a day do not know how to pity me."

Alferd G. Packer lived out the remainder of his life near Littleton, south of Denver; he died of a stroke in 1907.

One hundred and twenty years have passed since that dreadful winter of 1873-74, but interest in the Packer case has never faded. Generations of western history buffs have pondered the question of Packer's guilt. Did he, or did he not, actually murder the men he ate?

One man in particular took a very specific interest in that question. James Starrs, a law professor at George Washington University in Washington D.C., was fascinated by the fact that Packer was convicted almost entirely on circumstantial evidence. The physical evidence —the bodies themselves— had never been examined by trained professionals. As a forensic expert, Starrs wondered what a contemporary scientific analysis of the victims' bones would reveal.

In the early summer of 1989, Starrs announced with a great fanfare of publicity that he had assembled a team of forensic pathologists, anthropologists and archaeologists to exhume the gravesite.

The exhumation began with a sonar beam scan of the surface of the ground. Readings showed five places where the soil had been dug up and then replaced. By removing the earth a fraction of an inch at a time, the archaeologists uncovered and carefully brushed off five skeletons whose skulls bore unmistakable evidence of "multiple insults" in the form of hatchet wounds.

Examination of the bones determined which man was the youngest and which was oldest, thus identifying George Noon, 20, and Isreal Swan, 60. One of the skeletons had no skull, so this was believed to be Reddy Miller whose head was never found. The last two bodies were, of course, James Humphreys and Shannon Bell... but which was which?

Both skeletons showed evidence of defensive marks inflicted as the men tried to protect themselves while they were being killed. One victim had been savagely attacked, struck "indiscriminately and repeatedly with an axe-like instrument by someone who was, perhaps, in a wild rage." The other had also thrown up his arms to ward off the blows of his assailant.

On the basis of this evidence, Professor Starrs concluded Packer "'treated his five trusting companions as beasts of prey... he stripped them of their lives and their flesh and luxuriated in eating them."

However, in the minds of many who read the post-project conclusions, the exhumation did not clearly establish Packer's guilt. Packer may well have killed all five, but it remains equally possible that Bell killed the first four before losing his life in an attack on Packer. If Bell and Packer did indeed fight to the death, it is quite likely Packer struck Bell on the forearms before he succeeded in crushing his skull.

Undeniably there was incredible savagery at the end of this blood-curdling episode, but what really happened? What if Shannon Bell had been the one to walk out instead of Alferd Packer? What tale would he have told?

On Tuesday, August 15, 1990, the skeletons were reinterred in the original site following a memorial service conducted by four Lake City ministers. As dozens of cameras clicked away, more than 200 local citizens watched the lowering of a compartmentalized wooden box into the ground. After the hand-held ropes were drawn out of the grave, the dirt was shoveled back in on top of one of Colorado's favorite unsolved mysteries.

How to Visit the Site of the Alferd Packer Massacre

Lake City, 55 miles south of Gunnison, can be reached via State Highway 149. Drive through the town and go two miles further south on 149. The grave site is marked by a plaque mounted on a granite boulder on a bluff overlooking the Lake Fork River near Deadman's Gulch.

Throughout each summer, the Mountaineer Players of Western State College of Gunnison present a play, "The Last Trial of Alferd Packer," in the Hinsdale County courthouse where Packer was first tried in 1883. The famous cannibal's gourmandise is also celebrated annually with an Alferd Packer Barbecue. Exact dates for these events can be obtained from the Lake City Chamber of Commerce, P.O. Box 430, Lake City, CO 81235.

Bibliography - Chapter 5

Lake City Silver World, "Alferd Packer: New Discoveries, New Questions." Summer, 1990.

Gillette, Ethel. *Frontier Times* magazine. Austin, Texas. Western Publications. October, 1984.

Hill, Alice Polk. **Tales of the Colorado Pioneers.** Glorieta, New Mexico. The Rio Grande Press, Inc. 1976, reprint.

6

The Great Diamond Hoax

The two grubby prospectors looked completely out of place as they walked into the ornate foyer of the Bank of California in San Francisco that fine spring morning in 1872. Their clothes were tattered and dirty, and they obviously had not shaved or bathed for many days. They walked slowly and hesitantly across the shiny tiled floor, openly gawking at the white marble columns rising up to the high ceiling.

A teller in a dark suit eyed them with disdain. He was sure they had mistaken the bank for a saloon. He was about to tell them the nearest place for a beer was two blocks away when one of the men approached the teller's window and asked, "Are you a banker, sir?"

"I am an employee of this bank, yes," the teller replied stiffly.

"Well, sir," the scruffy fellow continued, "me an' my partner here got this little bag of diamonds that we'd like you to put in your vault for safe-keepin'. We figger it ain't a good idea to be walkin' around this town with diamonds in our pockets."

"Diamonds?" the teller responded with considerably more interest.

"Yes, sir. Here, I'll show you." The prospector plopped a small, grimy buckskin bag on the counter and pulled the drawstrings apart. The teller's eyes widened; he pushed up his glasses for a closer look. The sack did indeed contain diamonds... rough, uncut, unpolished, some still with dirt on them... but they certainly looked genuine.

The teller caught his breath and said, "Uh, wait right here, gentlemen. I'll be right back." He scurried off to the office of the bank's president, William C. Ralston. "Two men just brought in a pouch of diamonds, sir," he said. "I thought you would want to talk to them."

Ralston followed the teller back to his window, stared condescendingly at the raggedy prospectors and peered into the pouch. His stern expression vanished immediately. With a smile and a tone of respect, he said, "Welcome to the Bank of California, gentlemen. Please accompany me to my office where we can discuss how this bank may be of service to you."

Ralston ushered the awkward pair into his plush office. After closing the door, he beamed, "Well, introductions are in order. I am the president of this financial institution, and my name is William Ralston... but my closest friends call me Billy." He extended his hand. The first prospector quickly wiped his palm on his pantleg and shook hands politely.

"Pleased to meet you, Mister Billy, sir," he said. "My name is Jack Slack, and this here's my partner, Phillip Arnold. Me'n Philly been prospecting' together for, oh, probably 'bout five years now, ain't we, Philly? Well, we finally struck it rich. We found us a diamond field."

Ralston's eyes sparkled with an 18-carat gleam. "And where is this diamond field?" he asked.

"Why... uh, it's out in Arizona," Slack replied cautiously. "We're plannin' to go back pretty soon and do some more diggin'."

"Have your diamonds been appraised yet?" the banker asked. "No? Well, gentlemen, I think it would be in your best interest to know their true value. I can make arrangements to have them appraised, if you like."

"Why, that's down right nice of you, Mister Billy," Jack Slack said, with Philly Arnold bobbing his head in agreement.

The next morning, Ralston, Slack and Arnold took the gems to one of San Francisco's best jewelers who examined them and pronounced them to be "of excellent quality" with an estimated value of $125,000. As the trio walked back down the street, Slack said, "We sure do thank you for your help, Mister Billy. If you'll keep our jewels in your bank, we'll be headin' on out again to, huh, Arizona. We should be back before winter with another sack of diamonds bigger'n this one."

Ralston was tapping his chin with his forefinger as he walked along. "Gentlemen, I've been thinking," he said. "I believe it is quite possible there may be a much more profitable alternative open to you. True, you can continue to work your diamond field on your own and produce limited amounts of stones. On the other hand, with proper financial backing, a mining company could be formed which would have the resources needed for a full-scale commercial and professional development of your discovery.

"You two, of course, would be granted a substantial interest in this company and would enjoy the luxu-

ry of getting rich without having to do any back-break-
ing labor. The Bank of California would definitely be
interested in backing such an enterprise and, if you will
give me a few days, I feel quite certain I will have no
trouble locating additional investors. What do you say?"

"Mister Billy, you know more about financial
things than we do, but this sounds pretty good to me.
How 'bout you, Philly?" Phillip Arnold grinned oafishly
and nodded his consent.

William Ralston wasted no time in getting started. He quickly sent cables to two of his best friends:
Ashbury Harpending, a powerful financier who was
presently residing in London, and David D. Colton,
general manager of the Central Pacific Railroad. The
banker urged them to invest in this once-in-a-lifetime
opportunity.

Both men reacted skeptically; neither was willing
to put up any money until Ralston personally visited
the diamond field, verified its existence and produced
an assayer's report on its potential. Ralston explained
the situation to Slack and Arnold. He was adamant
that the three of them head off to Arizona at once.

The two prospectors glanced at one another.
Looking a little sheepish, Jack Slack said, "Mister Billy,
sir, I'm afraid we been fibbin' to you a little bit. Our
diamond field ain't really in Arizona. We just been
sayin' that so's nobody would know where it is. It's
really in Colorado. I hope you ain't mad at us."

Ralston laughed heartily. "Of course not. That's
splendid. Gentlemen, let's go to Colorado!"

A few days later, Slack and the taciturn Arnold
found themselves riding in a fancy compartment of a
Pullman car, smoking fine cigars with San Francisco's
leading investment banker. Accompanying them was
Henry Janin, a highly respected mining engineer whom

Ralston had hired to conduct a mineralization survey of the site when they reached it. The small group got off the train in Rock Springs, Wyoming, where they bought supplies and rented horses and a wagon.

From Rock Springs, they rode south on what is now State Road 430 and entered the northwestern corner of the Colorado territory. It was wild and rough country, but Slack and Arnold rode through it with confidence.

On the morning of the third day, Slack said, "I'm real apologetic about havin' to do this, Mister Billy and Mister Janin, but me'n Philly are gonna ask you to ride the rest of the way blindfolded. It ain't that we don't trust you, but we'd like to keep our strike a secret till we get all them papers signed and everythin'."

Ralston nodded. "That sounds like a prudent precaution. I have ridden in darkness before, and I have no fear of it . Go ahead, put on the blindfolds."

The group rode on for a few more miles before they halted and Slack said, "You can take off them bandanas now, gentlemen. Have yourselves a look around."

Their horses were standing on the edge of a wide, rocky dry wash across which a series of holes had been dug. "You can see where we done our diggin'," Slack pointed out. "The diamonds seem to be most plentiful downhill, but there's an awful lot of 'em right around here." He lifted a shovel out of the wagon. "Care to try your luck, Mister Billy?"

Ralston grasped the shovel and began digging a hole while Slack and Arnold crushed and sifted the dirt. They found nothing.

"Well," Arnold shrugged. "Just pick another spot."

Ralston walked a few paces and sunk his shovel

into the ground again. This time, as Slack and Arnold sifted the dirt, Arnold pointed and shouted, "There's one."

"Sure enough," Slack laughed. "Ol' eagle-eye Philly! It's just a little bitty one, but it's a start." Now Henry Janin peeled off his coat and joined the digging.

By late afternoon, the four men had unearthed a fair-sized handful of rough diamonds. Janin, perspiring heavily from his unaccustomed labor, declared, "I've never seen anything like this before. This area is rich beyond belief. It is the first —perhaps the only— major diamond field in America!"

William Ralston slung his sweaty arms around the two prospectors' shoulders. "My friends," he exulted, "This is a historic moment. I only wish we'd had the foresight to bring along some champagne. But there will be plenty of time for celebrations later. Mister Janin, when we get back to Rock Springs, I want you to continue on to New York. Have these jewels appraised at Tiffany's. That way we'll be absolutely certain of their true value. Jack and Philly and I will go back to San Francisco and await your return. Come back as quickly as possible. Get out those bandanas again, fellows, and let's be on our way."

The exploratory party rode off. Surely no two blindfolded men ever smiled as happily as Ralston and Janin did that day. Ralston's smile was especially wide; he knew that blindfold or no, he would have no trouble finding the diamond mine again.

Henry Janin made a hasty trip to New York City, where, according to most historic accounts, Charles Lewis Tiffany himself spread the diamonds out on the billiard table in his mansion. The renown jeweler scrutinized them carefully before announcing them to be worth $50,000. Tiffany then asked Janin if he would like to play a game of billiards.

They played a couple of games, but Janin was probably too excited to play well. He hastened back to San Francisco where he burst breathlessly into Ralston's office with the good news: "Tiffany says the diamonds are worth $50,000! Now, by my calculations, if four men can hand-dig that much in a single day, a commercial operation could produce over a million dollars a week!"

"Excellent news!" Ralston cried. "Excellent!" Then he paused and tapped his chin thoughtfully. "You know, it's probably best if Slack and Arnold know nothing about your report. I think I'll tell them a different story. They're good fellows, but there's really no place for them in a venture of this sort, and certainly no need to share millions with them now that we no longer need them.

"I imagine I can buy out their interests for a quarter of a million. No. I'll be generous. I'll make it $300,000. I'll take care of it first thing in the morning."

The next day, when Slack and Arnold entered the bank, Ralston put on his gloomiest expression and led the two men to his office. "I'm afraid I have bad news, my friends," he said. "Mister Janin has informed me that the productive potential of the diamond field will be much, much less than we anticipated. We plan to go ahead with the operation, if we can still find willing investors, but it will be years before our mining company shows a profit. I, as a banker, am used to making long-term investments with belated payoffs, but I imagine you two had hoped for an immediate cash return."

"We sure did, Mister Billy," said the crestfallen Jack Slack.

"Well, I'm not going to let you down," Ralston said firmly. "If you'd like to sell me your claim, I'm prepared to offer you $300,000 cash."

"Gosh Almighty," Slack beamed. "You hear that, Philly? Three hundred thousand apiece!"

Ralston winced, swallowed hard, and said, "Yes. Why... yes, of course, three hundred thousand apiece. I'll have the papers drawn up at once." Within an hour, Arnold and Slack carefully penned their signatures on an impressive looking document, solemnly shook hands with William C. Ralston and walked out of the Bank of California with $600,000 stuffed in their dirty, canvas bindle bags.

As soon as the two of them were back in their shabby hotel room, Phillip Arnold looked closely at himself in the mirror above the dresser. "Mister Slack," he said. "I believe the first thing we should do is buy ourselves some decent clothes. Quite frankly, I am sick and tired of going about dressed as a prospector."

"Oh, I heartily agree with you, Mister Arnold," Jack Slack concurred. "However, I think it is clearly in our best interest to seek a tailor in a different city. Let's get the hell out of San Francisco!"

Both men broke out laughing, slung their bags over their shoulders, and headed for the depot. Neither was ever seen in California again.

Meanwhile back at the bank, William Ralston was going into high gear. He formed the San Francisco and New York Mining and Commercial Company, selling interests in what was expected to be an enormous corporation capable of not only mining the gems but also cutting and marketing them worldwide. Ashbury Harpending invested heavily as did former presidential candidate George B. McClellen, New York Congressman B.F. Butler, Horace Greeley and Baron Rothschild.

The formation of this company rocked the financial world like an earthquake. A flood of high quality diamonds from the United States would impact every great financial center in Europe and might well ruin the economies of diamond producing countries such as South Africa and Brazil.

In the United States, speculation fever was running higher than it had since the discovery of the California gold fields 24 years earlier. Ralston was deluged with offers to buy stock in the mining company, but he wisely declined to put any stock on the market. He and his partners decided to develop only the original 3,000-acre claim and to hold onto the adjacent, marginal lands which by now they also controlled, until their value inevitably rose. These adjoining claims could then be sold on a cash and royalty basis to other entrepreneurs.

The nation's newspapers were full of speculations about the still-secret location of the Great American Diamond Fields. Ralston continued to insist they were in sandstone formations in Arizona. Most journalists accepted this story until word of Ralston's trip to Wyoming leaked out. Now, it was quite obvious the strike had been made somewhere south of Rock Springs.

One man who read these newspaper articles with particular interest was a young geologist named Clarence King. A brilliant, adventurous, Yale-educated surveyor, King was only 30 when he had been appointed director of the United States Geological Survey of the Fortieth Parallel. He and his 25-man survey crew spent more than two years systematically mapping the 1,000 mile long, 100-mile wide tract of the transcontinental railroad route. King's final report was one of the most comprehensive geologic and topographic studies

ever conducted in the western territories. In the mineralization section of his report, King emphasized that
the conditions for a major gemstone deposit did not
exist *anywhere* within the survey's study area.

Now suddenly he found himself reading outlandish newspaper accounts of a giant diamond strike
within the very same region he had explored so thoroughly. Was it possible he could have missed such a
bonanza? King did not think so for a minute. It was
quite clear to him that there was something very fishy
going on.

He hastily rounded up several members of his
original crew. They headed for Rock Springs, riding on
the railroad which traversed the route they themselves
had mapped just a few years earlier. It was late October; a fierce, early-winter wind greeted them as they
stepped off the train. It blasted them continuously as
they rode south, on horseback, through the bleak
country between Rock Springs and the Colorado line.
King experienced no trouble in locating the alleged diamond fields. A mere seven miles over the line, he found
the San Francisco and New York Mining and Commercial Company's claim marker and water rights notices
posted along the northern boundary.

The weather was worsening, so King and his
companions went right to work. Bracing themselves
against the wind, they began digging near the now-
eroded holes dug during Ralston's exploratory visit.
They found diamonds, of course, but not in places
where any knowledgeable prospector would expect to
find them.

The diamonds were all fairly close to the surface;
none appeared at the bedrock level where their high
specific gravity would have naturally caused them to
settle. King carefully examined each spadeful of earth

and noted that there was an almost pencil-thin column of disturbed dirt above each diamond in the otherwise pristine ground. The crew moved on downhill aways, dug more holes and found nothing. All of the diamonds seemed to be concentrated in a relatively small area.

Clarence King raised his face to the wind and breathed deeply. "I do believe I smell a whiff of fraud in the air," he said. "This so-called diamond field has been salted."

Once he was back in Rock Springs, King sent a lengthy telegram to William Ralston. Had Ralston not been such a hale and healthy man, he might well have suffered a heart attack when he read King's revelations. Instead, he simply slumped into his chair with the telegram crumpled in his hand, too stunned to even swear.

After the initial shock wore off, he slammed his desk with his fist, threw back his head and laughed out loud at the ironic nature of the hoax.

"Those two ornery rascals!" he guffawed. "They actually convinced me that *I* was taking *them* for a ride! Nicely done, gentlemen, but you won't get away with it!"

Ralston summoned Henry Janin to his office. "I have some painful news for you, Henry. I have been informed that our 'Great Colorado Diamond Field' is nothing but a hoax. We've been flim-flammed. So congratulations. You and I are about to become the two most ridiculed men in America. Our only consolation is that the illustrious Mister Charles Tiffany will share our embarrassment."

He smoothed out the crumpled telegram and handed it to Janin. The mining engineer's Adam's apple bobbed up and down as he read Clarence King's devastating report. "My God, Billy," Janin blurted out in a near-hysterical voice. "Everyone will think we were participants in this swindle. We'll be accused of being cohorts of Slack and Arnold. We could be indicted for fraud!"

"I think we can prove our honesty by returning every cent of our investors' money," Ralston said. "The $600,000 that was lost will, I'm afraid, have to come out of my own pocket. And then I'm going to spend some more of my own money to hire some detectives. I'll find those two scoundrels no matter where they have gone!"

In the days that followed, Ralston and Janin did indeed become the laughingstock of San Francisco. From the brokerage houses to the saloons, everyone was joking about their gullibility. A lot of people were drinking toasts to the improbable pair who had humbled them.

William Ralston put the Pinkerton Detective Agency on the trail of the missing con men. Investigators had no trouble learning a great deal about Jack Slack and Phillip Arnold. They discovered that Arnold had once worked at the San Francisco Diamond Drill Company where he became familiar with industrial-grade diamonds and their sources. Slack was a small time gold prospector who had for the most part enjoyed only marginal luck. Where these two men met and when they teamed up could not be established, but they had eventually gone prospecting together and had made a pretty respectable gold strike. Reportedly, they sold their claim for $50,000.

Their next step was a trip to Amsterdam, where Arnold bought somewhere between $35,000 and $50,000 worth of low quality African reject-diamonds. The gem wholesalers remembered him well, for they wondered at the time why his seemingly astute man was solely interested in dirt-cheap diamonds which had only the appearance of being good ones.

Upon their return to the United States, Arnold and Slack traveled west to pick a site for their "diamond field." They chose the obscure dry wash in northern Colorado for several reasons. The locale was relatively remote and untouched, but was still fairly close to the railroad, and there was a reliable source of water nearby. It was a very enticing place for a mining operation had there really been anything there to mine.

They first criss-crossed the area with a pattern of holes to make it look as if they had actually explored the gully. Then they moved out beyond the holes and carefully pushed metal rods a few feet into the soil. Into each of these tiny shafts, they dropped an inexpensive diamond, then painstakingly brushed loose dirt in on top of it.

Once the area had been "salted" with half of the diamonds, the wily pair headed for San Francisco with the other half in a little buckskin pouch. They really had nothing to lose; if no one in San Francisco fell for their scheme, they could always retrieve their diamonds and resell them at the price they had originally paid. Surely both men were pleasantly surprised to learn so quickly there would be no need to do so.

The ease with which Arnold and Slack duped Billy Ralston is probably understandable. Ralston was an investment banker, a man who dealt in dollars, gold and real estate; he had no expertise in the mining of gemstones. Perhaps Henry Janin, too, can be excused for his misjudgment. As a mining engineer, he was quite knowledgeable about silver and gold fields, but he had never seen a diamond field.

Charles Tiffany's failure to recognize the diamond's real value is much harder to explain. Why did the nation's number one jeweler appraise a handful of industrial diamonds at more than three times their true worth? One explanation may be that Tiffany was accustomed to examining finely cut, highly polished jewels; he rarely, if ever, touched raw, fresh-out-of-the-ground diamonds. Or possibly he was simply more interested in shooting billiards that evening.

After Slack and Arnold made their hasty departure from San Francisco, they parted company. Apparently they were wise enough to quit while they were ahead. It is likely they never saw one another again. Jack Slack simply disappeared; his whereabouts remained unknown until his death by natural causes 24 years later in White Oaks, New Mexico.

Phillip Arnold returned to his native Kentucky where he bought a large country estate, built a fine house and lived the life of a southern aristocrat. He made no attempt to hide the fact that he had gained his money by swindling a Yankee banker. In fact, he loved to boast about it. In Kentucky, as throughout the post-Civil War South, hatred of Yankees still ran very high, and Arnold came to be regarded as a folk hero.

The Pinkertons had no difficulty locating Arnold but arresting him and extraditing him proved to an entirely different matter. The State of Kentucky flatly refused extradition. It is said that armed groups of local citizens surrounded Arnold's estate to chase off anyone attempting to serve a warrant.

Back in San Francisco, Ralston filed a personal damages suit against Arnold for $300,000. After a long legal battle, Arnold agreed to an out-of-court settlement to avoid further litigation. Some historians claim he returned $150,000, while others contend it was only $30,000, a mere ten cents on the dollar.

Billy Ralston's life was never the same. His previous investors no longer trusted his judgement, his prestige in the financial centers of San Francisco evaporated. On August 25, 1875, the board of directors of the Bank of California demanded his resignation. On August 26, his lifeless body was fished out of San Francisco Bay. He left no suicide note, but no one doubted he had taken his own life.

Out in the Colorado "diamond field," the dry gulch had derisively been named Diamond Wash Draw. The mountain above it was "Diamond Peak," and one of the area's streams came to be called Arnold Creek. It may be the people who gave names to these landmarks felt a bit of pity for Billy Ralston, for they were kind enough not to name anything in the area after him.

How to Visit the "Colorado Diamond Fields"

After reaching the Wyoming-Colorado state line on State Highway 430 from Rock Springs, continue south three-quarters of a mile to a Y-junction. Turn right and watch for a turn-off onto an unimproved dirt road approximately a quarter of a mile on south on the right. This road travels west around 9,545-foot Diamond Peak at the 8,000-foot level. The area that was salted with diamonds lies north of this road between the junction and Diamond Peak itself.

This same destination can be reached from Maybell, Colorado by taking the Cherokee Park Trail road to the previously mentioned junction three-quarters of a mile below the state line.

Bibliography - Chapter 6

King, Clarence. **Moutaineering in the Sierra Nevada.**
    Layton, Utah. Peregrine Smith, Inc. 1983
    reprint.

Merritt, J.L. *American West* magazine. Tucson. Ameri-
    can West Publishing Company. July-August,
    1982.

Norton, Allen. *True West* magazine. Austin, Texas.
    Western Publications. July-August, 1957.

Voynick, Steve. *True West* magazine. Austin, Texas.
    Western Publications. January, 1989.

Williams, Brad and Pepper, Choral. **The Mysterious
    West.** Cleveland, Ohio. World Publishing Com-
    pany. 1967.

7

Felipe Espinosa's
Reign of Terror

Spring had barely come to the high country when the first mutilated body was found.

The naked corpse lay sprawled, stark and white, across the muddy wheel-rut of the wagon track that served as a road along the Arkansas River between Parksdale and Cotopaxi. The victim was young, male and had been butchered savagely, apparently with an axe. His chest had been hacked open, his ribs slashed away, and his heart was torn out. The cowboy who discovered the body immediately spurred his horse back to Parksdale to report the murder.

At this time, May, 1863, Fremont County, Colorado was sparsely populated, so it was not easy to round up a posse to ride back to the scene of the crime. But soon a handful of local citizens galloped off to retrieve the body. After those gentle townsfolk recovered from their initial shock, they lifted the victim onto a blanket, wrapped him up and placed him in the bed of a horse-drawn wagon.

None of these citizens were law enforcement investigators or man-hunting trackers, but they inspected the site as best they could. There were plenty of footprints in the mud and everyone agreed at least three assailants participated in the atrocity. The young man's clothing was found behind a boulder in the steep-walled canyon. In the pockets were the victim's wallet, money and watch. He had not been robbed. The papers he carried identified him as a member of the territorial militia.

The only conclusion that townspeople could draw was that "somebody sure must have hated that poor boy."

The next victim was a man who no one in Fremont County hated. William Bruce was a kindly, well-respected old fellow who ran a saw mill on Hardscrabble Creek, not far from the site of the first killing. Everyone called him "Judge" because he had a certain judicial look about him.

A few days after the original murder, Judge Bruce rode off toward town to conduct a bit of business. When he did not return, his wife organized some of her neighbors to search for him. They found his body lying on the roadside less than ten miles from his home. He had been shot between the eyes. The powder burns on his face indicated that the bullet was fired as a *coup de grace*, at point blank range, after which his clothes had been stripped off and his heart chopped out.

Before the end of the month, the naked body of a reclusive elderly man, Henry Hawkins, was recovered from the banks of Fountain Creek near the spot where Henry always dipped his bucket to draw his drinking water. He, too, had been shot and mutilated.

The month of May was a time of numbing shock for the citizens of Fremont County, but June turned out to be an absolute nightmare for the whole region.

The next murder occurred near Fairplay, nearly 70 miles north of the site of the first killings. Judging by the condition of the corpse, it was obviously the work of the same savage fiends. Within days, a rancher named Addleman was found dead in a pasture in the same vicinity. While posses searched the Fairplay area, the killers were already miles away, setting up an ambush on the road to Leadville.

The first two men to ride into this deadly trap were a pair of young cowboys, Nelson Shoup and Tom Brinkley. Shoup was killed instantly by the triangulated rifle fire that burst from concealed positions in the rocks above the road. Brinkley was knocked from his horse by a bullet through the shoulder. He dragged himself into the brush and crawled away, desperately seeking a place to hide.

While one member of the gang stayed on the road to tear off Shoup's clothing and whack open his chest with powerful strokes from a long-handled axe, the other assailants fanned out into the brush searching for Tom Brinkley.

As the wounded cowboy listened to the chopping sounds coming from the road, he crept into some rocks and tried not to make a sound. It was all in vain. The killers soon found him, drug him out by his heels and shot him through the forehead. After they had ripped off his shirt, the tall man with the axe strode down the slope, stepped straddle-legged over the corpse and began swinging.

Once Brinkley's heart had been hewn from his chest, the axe-wielder and his accomplices returned to their original positions in the rocks, reloaded their rifles and waited for the next traveler to come down the trail.

Around noon, George Carter rode into the killers' gunsights. He was blown away, chopped up and thrown into the bushes. As the murderers were disposing of Carter's remains, they heard the heavy creak of approaching wagon wheels. There was no time to return to the ambush sites, so the gang raced out into the road and blazed away wildly at the passing wagon.

The teamster, Henry Metcalf, was hauling a large wagonload of sawed lumber drawn by four yoke of oxen. Most of the bullets thudded into the piled boards; Metcalf sustained only a superficial injury. He slapped the reins frantically, popped his whip and forced the plodding beasts into a near gallop. He expected to be pursued, but was not. Perhaps, as he speculated afterwards, the killers had tethered their horses too far away to be able to mount up for an immediate chase.

In any event, Metcalf became the first person to escape from the demonic marauders, and the first to have gotten a look at them. He reported seeing three men whose faces were blackened with soot to make them unrecognizable.

By now everyone living between Leadville and Canon City was in a state of near-panic. No one could be sure where these sadistic, diabolical phantoms would strike next. After the Leadville rampage, several more butchered bodies showed up along the Arkansas River road. Why? What kind of demons were scouring the land in search of victims?

Few were foolish enough to travel alone anymore. Those who dared to venture out in groups always rode forth heavily armed. Many miners, ranchers and even businessmen stepped forward to be deputized, joining the local law officers in their futile searches of the mountainous terrain. The territorial governor, John Evans, enlarged the Colorado militia and ordered them to take part in the manhunt. Still, no clues to the murderers' identities could be found, nor could any possible motive be determined.

Despite these efforts, the gang of butchers continued to strike again and again in isolated areas. By the end of July 1863, more than 20 men had been slain, all in the same horrible manner.

Emotions were now running so high that people were being endangered in other ways. One morning, John Foster, a hotel owner, walked out of Fairplay to check on the well being of a friend who lived in a cabin near town. As he rounded a bend in the road, a group of horsemen came galloping toward him. Terrified, Foster ran into the woods and the horsemen who were members of one of the posses, pursued him on the assumption that he was one of the killers.

The portly hotelier raced for his life through the pines, dodging and ducking as the lawmen fired away at him. He ran to the nearest house and was pounding on the door when the officers pounced on him. They pummeled poor Foster with their fists and were starting to tie a hangman's knot in a rope when the local Methodist minister, John Dyer, arrived shouting, "In the name of God—stop! This man is a member of my congregation."

The posse apologized for their mistake and rode on. The next man to be mistaken for a killer was not so lucky.

George Baxter was sighted by a posse near the site of one of the killings. Baxter, like Foster, made the mistake of running. The law officers chased him down and promptly hanged him on the spot. It was not until the next day that the hot-headed posse members realized they had lynched an innocent man.

Colorado's bloody summer of 1863 had now entered August. Local authorities were no closer to ending the carnage than they had been in May. They still had no idea who was perpetrating the crimes nor why.

Then one day, Governor Evans received a very strange letter. A chill ran up the back of his neck as he read it. He read it a second time, leaned back in his chair with a frown on his face and muttered, "My god, what kind of man would write such a letter?"

The letter began:

"Your Excellency,

"We have cut the hearts out of 26 American dogs so far but we are willing to forgo further slaughter if you will grant me and my followers full pardons and permit us to retain 5000 acres we now claim in Conejos County with the free use of all adjacent grazing lands and that you will appoint me and any of my followers whom I may designate as captains in the Colorado Volunteers.

"For these things we will desist from further molestation of your subjects. I will give you until the end of September to do these things and if it is not done, 574 more gringos will die. Among them will be yourself."

The letter was signed: "Felipe Nerio Espinosa."

The governor stroked his long, white chin whiskers. Was this some sort of morbid joke? Surely no one in his right mind would make such preposterous demands.

And why had the writer chosen to use such precise figures? True, 26 murders had been reported so far; that was common knowledge available to almost anyone, but how had the figure 574 been selected? Why was the final possible death toll set at exactly 600 victims?

Governor Evans stared hard at the signature of Felipe Nerio Espinosa. Espinosa was a common name in southern Colorado. The whole thing sounded like a hoax, but at that time no stone could be left unturned. Evans immediately sent a telegram to Emmett Harding, sheriff of Conejos County, requesting that he search for and apprehend Felipe Espinosa as a prime suspect in the Fremont, Lake and Park County murders.

Sheriff Harding, accompanied by deputies, rode off to question residents of the scattered Hispanic communities around and along the Conejos River. From them he learned that a man named Felipe Espinosa had indeed once lived in the area. The people who knew him had disliked him and were more than a little afraid of him for he constantly boasted about being an outlaw. No one was sorry to see him go when he left the valley.

Someone suggested the sheriff should talk to the local priest since he might well have additional information.

"Si," the good padre replied when Sheriff Harding called upon him. "I remember Felipe Espinosa. He is a very troubled man. Come in. I will tell you about him."

Felipe Nerio Espinosa, the priest said, was born in Vera Cruz, Mexico. He was still quite young when the Mexican-American War broke out in 1846. During the bloody conflict the U.S. Navy bombarded Vera Cruz for two days, firing 1,300 shells, most of which exploded in residential neighborhoods.

Young Felipe was apparently away from his home

when the bombardment commenced. After the shelling ceased, he went back to his *barrio* and found his house and the house of his grandparents destroyed. The bodies of his parents, his grandparents, and his brother and sister had been carried, along with scores of others, to the Convent of Santo Domingo where they lay beneath sheets awaiting identification.

Felipe Espinosa, with a nun standing supportively beside him, knelt on the cold, stone floor and lifted the sheets, one by one. Each corpse he unveiled was mangled and torn almost beyond recognition, but he was able to identify the bodies of each of the six dearest people in his life.

The only relatives he had left were two cousins living far away in a part of the land that had previously been northern Mexico, but was now called the U.S. Territory of New Mexico. The cousins sent for Felipe. At the age of 12 or 13, the boy went north to live with them.

He never recovered from his grief. Almost nightly he tossed and turned in his bed reliving in frightful dreams the horror of lifting blood-stained sheets from the broken bodies of his loved ones.

As he worked in his cousins' fields, he often saw blue-coated American soldiers riding arrogantly by on the roads. He watched as more and more Anglos moved onto formerly Hispanic lands, claiming them for themselves. By the time Felipe reached his late teens, his grief had turned to anger.

"The gringos are stealing everything from us," he lamented to his cousins. "They stole the lives of my entire family. Now they are stealing the very lands our people live on. If they steal from us, is it not fair —and just— for us to steal from them?"

Tired of living in poverty, the cousins agreed and

shortly thereafter, probably in 1855, Felipe, Victorio and Julian became horse thieves.

The priest's story continued, explaining how the young men had come to Conejos County. They stole horses and mules from Anglo ranchers in New Mexico, drove them north into Colorado and sold them in the booming mining camps. Within a couple of years, the Espinosas moved their lucrative rustling operation to Conejos County and began selling stolen beef to the hungry miners.

Felipe's cousins were quite satisfied with their new lives, but for Felipe himself, it was nowhere near enough. The young outlaw enjoyed stealing from people he considered to be his enemies, but what he really wanted was vengeance. A fiery rage burned within him, and his nightmares were growing worse. One night he had a dream so vivid, he went to talk to a priest the next morning.

He told the padre he had had a vision. The Virgin Mary had come to him and commanded him to kill 100 Americans for each of his slain relatives. He wished to kneel at the altar and make a vow to do so.

"I absolutely refused to let him make such a blasphemous commitment in this holy church," the padre told Sheriff Harding. "I tried to explain to him that it could not have been the Blessed Virgin who came to him in his dream. It was the Devil, tricking him. But he would not listen. Or perhaps he could not listen. If you had seen the unholy gleam in his eyes, you would understand. He went away, and I have not seen him since."

After the sheriff passed this information along to Governor Evans, the governor announced the Territory of Colorado was offering a dead-or-alive reward of $2,500 for Felipe Nerio Espinosa. At long last, the lawmen and the militia volunteers knew the identities of the men they were hunting, but that did not make it much easier to find the outlaws. Even though the enticing reward lured scores of amateur bounty hunters to the mountains and river valleys around Fairplay and Leadville, the sadistic gang remained as elusive as ever.

"Damn it!" roared Colonel S.B. Tappan, commander of the Colorado Volunteers during a staff meeting with his fellow officers. "Isn't there *anyone* in this territory who knows how to track down outlaws? Everyone's out there running around like a bunch of nitwits. Surely there is someone, somewhere, who is capable of locating this pack of maniacs and bringing them to justice!"

A young lieutenant, Harold W. Baldwin, cleared his throat. "Beg pardon for interrupting you, sir, but I believe I know of such a man. You may remember him. His name is Thomas Tobin."

The colonel stopped pacing the floor. "Tobin," he said. "He used to be one of our scouts, didn't he?"

"Best we ever had, sir," Baldwin replied. "And before that he lived the life of a mountain man. If you'll forgive a bit of impiety, sir, the men used to say Tom Tobin could have followed Jesus Christ's footprints after he walked across the water."

"And where is Mister Tobin nowadays?" the colonel asked.

"I've heard he's taken up farming; he has a little spread along the South Platte. Would you like me to talk to him, sir?"

"The sooner the better," the colonel ordered. "Go at once."

Lieutenant Baldwin arrived at Thomas Tobin's farm the next afternoon. Tobin had obviously been

TOM TOBIN. A retired manhunter who took up his gun one last time to track down Colorado's deadliest killers.

watching him from the moment he and his horse appeared on the horizon. He was standing on his porch, waiting. "Well, Harold," Tobin said. "I don't imagine you rode all the way out here to talk about the weather. Get down off your horse and come on inside."

After the two men had seated themselves at the kitchen table in Tobin's unpretentious cabin, Baldwin said, "I'll get right to the point, Tom. We need your help in tracking down the Espinosas."

"I don't hunt men anymore," Tobin replied.

Baldwin studied the ex-scout's expressionless face. Tobin was still a fairly young man, probably less than 40, but his eyes were those of a much older man, a man who had seen far too much bloodshed. Baldwin chose his words carefully as he said, "That gang's got to be stopped, Tom. Without your help, there's no telling how long it will take or how many more people will die. Colonel Tappan is willing to place a full company of militia at your disposal, more than that if you need them."

Tobin scoffed at the offer. "You want me to go out with all them soldier-boys clankin' and clatterin' along behind me? I wouldn't get within ten miles of the outlaws." He fell silent for a moment, then said, "Tell you what I'll do, Harold. I'll track down your killers for you, but I want two, no more'n three soldiers riding along. Keep them troopers back in their barracks, and for Christ's sake, get all them damn-fool vigilantes off the roads."

Lieutenant Baldwin stood up from his chair. "I knew you'd come through for us, Tom. And, if I may, I'd like to be one of those three soldiers who ride with you."

"Suits me,"' Tobin shrugged as he lifted his long-barreled, muzzle-loading rifle off its rack on the wall.

Quickly Baldwin said, "I'll personally make sure

you are issued a better rifle, a brand new Sharps."

"This here's the only one I've ever needed," Tobin responded. He slung the ancient firearm loosely over his shoulder. "Let's go talk to that colonel of yours."

Late the next day, Tobin and Baldwin rode into Fairplay where Colonel Tappan immediately spread a map in front of them and jabbed his finger at the "X" he had inked in near Coaldale. "The 28th body was found here a couple of days ago. My men followed the killers' tracks as far as the river and lost the trail there."

"Harold," Tobin said. "How long'll it take you to pick out two troopers, get them outfitted and mounted up? I want to ride out of here before sundown."

Tobin, Baldwin and two enlisted men were in their saddles within an hour; they rode throughout the night, reaching the murder scene just at dawn. Tobin studied the area carefully. "Them soldier-boys left a hell of a lot more tracks than them outlaws did," he observed. "But, it's still plain enough that there was only three of them. Their horses ain't been shod in quite a while, and their boots're gettin' a little rundown."

He pointed to a faint pair of footprints. "This fella here, judging by the length of his stride, is the tallest in the bunch. He's also the one that straddled the body and done the choppin'. Let's go on up the road and see what else we can find."

Within a mile, the four riders easily located the spot where the killers left the road and headed for the South Platte. When they halted their horses on the bank of the smooth-flowing river, Lieutenant Baldwin said, "Small wonder the troopers couldn't follow the gang beyond this point. There's no way of telling where they went from here."

"They went upstream," Tobin said. "See how

some of them stones been pushed down in the sand. They rode their horses into the water and headed north. All we gotta do now is find the place where they come back out."

He nudged his horse into the shallow water and carefully guided the reluctant animal forward against the current. Nearly an hour went by before Baldwin, who was splashing along behind, shouted, "There!" He pointed at a set of hoofprints that had crumbled the edge of the riverbank. "They came out right there!"

"That's just what they wanted you to think, Harold," Tobin responded. "Them hoofprints was made by horses that was rode up the bank and backed down again. Let's cross over to the other side. I think we'll find us somethin' more interestin' to look at."

When the riders reached the opposite shore, Tobin said, "You fellas wait here a little while." He rode slowly on upstream, intently eyeing the shoreline. Soon he paused, turned around and beckoned to Baldwin. The lieutenant hurriedly sloshed up to his side.

"Here's where they left the river," said Tobin. "It's plain as day."

Baldwin was stumped. "I don't see anything."

"That's because they tried to brush away their tracks with pine branches. We shouldn't have no trouble trackin' them from here on. I expect they figure they've lost anybody who's tried to follow them, so now they won't worry as much about leavin' signs."

For the next two days, Tobin and the soldiers moved steadily through the piney forests and aspen groves northwest of the South Platte. Baldwin never ceased to marvel at the keenness of Tobin's eyes. The scout never seemed to miss the faintest track, broken twig or overturned stone. Only when daylight was completely gone would he stop for the night.

On the morning of the third day, the trail led to a small meadow. Tobin halted his horse at the edge of it. In the heavy timber beyond the grassy area, a flock of magpies had settled into the treetops. Tobin watched the birds intently for several minutes. Then, with a satisfied grin, he said, "Boys, I do believe we have finally found us them outlaws' camp."

He swung down from his saddle. The puzzled soldiers did the same. "We'll leave the horses here and circle around the meadow through the trees," Tobin said. "If everybody keeps real quiet, I think them desperados are in for quite a surprise."

The four men moved off silently through the pines, stepping lightly and staying in the shadows. Just before they reached the magpie-filled trees, Tobin crouched in the brush and whispered, "Can you smell it, Harold?"

"Smell what?"

"Fresh meat," Tobin replied. "That's what drew in them magpies." He parted the brush with his hand, and there, a stone's throw away, stood a scraggly-bearded man slicing thin strips of beef from a steer carcass. The man hung the meat on tree branches to dry.

One of the enlisted men sprang to his feet. "That varmint ain't gonna live long enough to eat that jerky!" he shouted. He fired his rifle and sent the rustler spinning head over heels across the ground. The mortally wounded man rose up screaming, "Felipe! Julian! *Escaparse! Me mataron!*"

"Damn you, sergeant!" Tobin roared. "Now we got us a shoot out on our hands instead of an ambush!"

In the same instant, a second bearded man stepped out from behind a tree and fired at the soldiers. As the troopers dove for cover, Tobin raised his muzzle-loader and sent a lead ball thudding into the outlaw's chest.

Now Felipe Espinosa himself burst from the tree-line and ran wildly across the meadow. "Bring him down!" Tobin yelled as he quickly crammed powder and a ball in his rifle. "Drop him!"

Baldwin fired and missed. Espinosa was nearly halfway across the meadow when Tobin elevated his muzzle-loader and pulled the trigger. The lead ball arched through the air and landed in the center of Espinosa's back, breaking it just below the short ribs.

Felipe Espinosa tried to get up but when he could not, he propped himself on his elbows and glared at the approaching Tobin.

The scout knelt beside the outlaw and drew his Bowie knife from its scabbard. "I hope your knife is sharp, gringo." Espinosa sneered.

"It is," Tobin replied matter of factly. He grabbed a handful of the killer's hair, bent his head back and slit his throat. The horrific gleam of madness did not fade from Felipe Espinosa's hate-filled eyes until he had been completely decapitated. While the lieutenant vomited in the grass, Thomas Tobin carried the head by its hair back to the horses and stuffed it in a burlap sack.

Felipe Nerio Espinosa's reign of terror was over at last, but since no member of the murderous gang was taken alive, it will never be known why the cousins participated in the madman's rampage. Did they really believe Felipe had experienced a vision? Could it be that they actually thought Felipe's wild scheme to acquire ranchlands in Conejos County and officer commissions in the militia would succeed? Or were they simply so afraid of him that Victorio and Julian dared not incur his wrath by refusing to be his accomplices?

Such questions remain forever unanswered.

A few days after the high country shoot out, Thomas Tobin arrived at the State Capitol in Denver, carrying his blood-encrusted sack. The startled governor rose from behind his desk. "Oh, Mister Tobin," he stammered. "Come in, please. Uh, you needn't bring that sack into my office. Just leave it in the hallway. That'll be fine."

After Tobin dropped the sack, Governor Evans went on to say, "Well, Thomas, you've certainly done this territory a great service. A good piece of work, I must say. May I offer you a cigar?"

Tobin shook his head. "I just came in to pick up the reward."

Evans stroked his beard nervously. "Thomas, I'm afraid there's, huh... a bit of a problem. My offer of a reward was made in good faith, but I was later informed that there is no money available in the territorial treasury to pay it. I... I'm terribly sorry."

The governor glanced down from Tobin's still expressionless face and looked at the farmer's ragged, threadbare coat. Evans' eyes brightened. "Well, the least I can do is buy you a new jacket at my own expense. After all, we want you to look your best when you have your picture taken for posterity."

Two hours later, Thomas Tobin, wearing a beaded buckskin coat, a new white shirt and a brocaded vest, posed for a photographer. Then he rode back out of town. He left his gunny sack at the Colorado Volunteers' headquarters in Fort Garland and returned to his farm.

Felipe Espinosa's head, which was undoubtedly in rather ghastly condition by this time, was preserved in a jar of alcohol. It was finally sold to a traveling carnival. For many years thereafter, thousands of curiosity seekers stared into his blank, baleful eyes, shuddered and went away, hoping they would not be awakened by those eyes in their dreams.

How to Follow Felipe Espinosa's Trail of Terror

Although none of the Espinosa ambush sites can be specifically identified today, a majority of them occurred on the Arkansas River road between Salida and Canon City. As one drives on U.S. Highway 50 through this scenic 60 mile, steep-walled canyon today, it is easy to understand how the Espinosas were able to bushwhack the unwary. Almost every curve in the road reveals a potential place for the concealment of murderous riflemen. One cannot help but shudder at the thought of riding alone through this canyon in 1863.

Bibliography - Chapter 7

Hewitt, Edgar L. *The Colorado Magazine.* Denver. The State Historical Society. January, 1931.

Kildare, Maurice. *Great West* magazine. New York. M.F. Enterprises. December, 1972.

Priest, Henry. *The Colorado Magazine.* Denver. The State Historical Society. January, 1931.

Simmons, Virginia McConnel. **The San Luis Valley, Land of the Six-Armed Cross.** Boulder, Colorado. Pruett Publishing Company. 1979.

Thorp, Raymond W. *Frontier Times* magazine. Western Publications. Austin, Texas. October-November, 1964.

8

"You Can't Trust Anybody Nowadays"

The gold rush was over and the Oro City boom was busted.

Once-crowded streets of this ramshackle, improbable town perched high on a hill in the rugged Sawatch Mountains were all but deserted. The shanties, tents and cabins that had housed more than 5,000 men and a handful of women during Oro City's brief heyday stood empty, inhabited now only by the cold, relentless wind.

Oro City was born in 1860 on the day a scrawny little prospector named Abe Lee picked through the washings in his gold pan, looked up at his pals and said, "Boys, I've got all of California right here in this pan!"

News of Lee's fantastic gold strike spread across and beyond Colorado like a crown-fire in an alpine forest. Prospectors and claim jumpers, entrepreneurs and con artists raced into this soaring wilderness at an average of 200 a week. Everyone believed that a new Comstock gold field had been discovered, so the whole region soon came to be called California Gulch.

Between 1860 and 1863, the gulch's floors and hillsides produced somewhere between five and ten million dollars in gold. Eventually, the placers washed out; the gold was all gobbled up and gone. Nearly everyone moved away to search for more lucrative locales.

Only a few die-hards lingered on in California Gulch, scavenging through the mine tailings and sifting the "leavings" of the abandoned mines. At first, these hard scrabblers were able to pan out about two dollars a day, which was not an unreasonable reward for their efforts considering that this was twice the going wage paid laborers at that time.

But inevitably the pickings grew slimmer. Earnings dropped to a dollar a day, then to fifty cents. Men began to drift on out.

One of the few who stayed was a young man named Sam Harris, a drought-busted farmer from Missouri. Sam had been washing gravel in a small, untouched side canyon beyond the main mines. This little tributary had gone undeveloped during the boom years because it was not rich enough to justify commercial investment. However, as Sam Harris discovered, one man working alone up there could, on a good day, pan out nearly four dollars worth of golden flakes.

As Harris gradually and thoroughly explored his canyon, he occasionally noticed deposits of an odd, black sand. Out of curiosity, he bagged a sample and took it with him on one of his periodic trips to Denver.

After he had converted his small pouch of gold to cash, he took his sack of black sand to an assayer's office. The metallurgist, Jonas Emerson, made a routine test. "Good Lord," he said. "This can't be right. I must have made a mistake. Let me run a second test."

When he had done so, Emerson looked up at Sam Harris excitedly. In an awed voice, he said, "There's no mistake. Mr. Harris, this sand is very nearly pure carbonate of lead with a higher silver concentrate than I have ever seen in my life."

Emerson scribbled hurriedly on a piece of paper. "At the current price of silver, I'd say this sand is worth nearly $4,000 a ton. Have you filed a claim yet?"

When Harris shook his head, Emerson said, "I strongly urge you to do so as soon as possible. But, not on the sand. What you must do now is locate the rocks this sand came from. Find those rocks, Mister Harris, and you'll be one of the richest men in Colorado."

Sam Harris wasted no time in riding back to his lonely canyon. He had no trouble finding the ore-laden rocks which were the source of the black sand again, so he quickly raced back to Denver and filed a claim. Next, he took the assayer's report and his samples to the office of the Colorado Mining and Mineral Corporation where he told the story of his discovery to J.F. Matthews, the corporation's president.

Matthews immediately realized Harris had stumbled onto a true bonanza and he definitely wanted in on it. "If this corporation was willing to buy your claim, what would be your asking price?" he inquired.

"One hundred thousand dollars," Harris replied. "Plus one-third of the profits. That's the least I would consider."

Rather than risk having Harris go to another mining company, Matthews promptly agreed. "I'll turn these samples and Emerson's report over to our own assayers," he said. "And if you will draw us a map of your claim, I'll send a field team out to inspect it. Once they have verified its potential, we'll sign the agreement we have just discussed. It'll take a few weeks, of course, so in the meantime, relax and enjoy Denver, Mr. Harris."

Harris checked into an inexpensive hotel and spent a few days taking in the sights. He was, however, much too excited to pass his time just rambling around town. He decided to go back to California Gulch and see for himself how the mineral survey was progressing. When he arrived in his little canyon, he had no more than gotten down from his horse when four rough-looking men stepped out of the trees and pointed rifles at him. "You got two minutes to get off this claim," said the meanest-looking one.

Keeping his hands well away from his own gun, Harris said, "This is my claim. It's on file in Denver."

All four men laughed and the one with the hard eyes said, "That ain't what we was told when Mister Matthews hired us to guard this piece of land. You're trespassing on the property of the Colorado Mining and Mineral Corporation. And you got less'n one of them minutes left."

Sam Harris swung back in his saddle and rode away. He made the long, hard ride back to Denver as quickly as possible. When he stormed into the courthouse, he was informed that there was no record at all of a Samuel Bedford Harris ever having filed a mining claim. There was, instead, a Colorado Mining and Mineral Corporation claim to the mineral rights in Harris' canyon.

The stunned Harris hastened over the Jonas Emerson's office. Surely, he thought, the assayer could at least verify that he had tested his samples and written a report for him,

SAM HARRIS. Was this drought-busted Missouri farmer cheated out of a fortune in silver by the Colorado Mining and Mineral Corporation?

Sam Harris nearly fell on the floor when Emerson said, "What did you say your name is? Harris? Well, Mister Harris, I'm sorry, but I've never seen you before today."

Now Harris' shock turned to anger. He stomped out of Emerson's door and headed directly to a law firm on Broadway Avenue. As soon as he seated himself in front of attorney Jerod Flemming's desk, he said, "I've been swindled, and I want justice."

Flemming listened intently as Harris explained. Then he leaned back in his chair and nodded knowingly. "Yep, that sure sounds like something J.F. Matthews would pull off. He's a very slick and unscrupulous man, Mister Harris. Obviously he bribed someone to remove your claim from the files and to replace it with one of his own. He also paid old Jonas to deny he had assayed your samples."

"Damn," Harris, mumbled. "You can't trust anybody nowadays."

"If you wish, I can file a suit on your behalf," Flemming went on. "But frankly, it'll be a long, uphill fight. You have no supportive evidence whatsoever to back your claim to those minerals and even if you did Matthews' lawyers could tie the case up in the courts for years."

"Forget it then," Harris sighed. "I wouldn't have the money to pay you. In fact, what I need more than anything right now is a job. Thanks for your time, Mister Flemming."

A few days later, Sam Harris went to work as a bartender in the Golden Slipper saloon on Larimer Street. Like all bartenders, he heard a lot of stories while he worked. His bitterness deepened as he listened to the tales about the fantastic California Gulch silver rush.

The Colorado Mining and Mineral operation was a tremendous success. The just-below-the-surface deposits were yielding thousands of dollars daily. The deep underground shafts being bored promised to produce millions. J.F. Matthews had named his mine the Silver Lady, and was managing it personally.

At least a dozen other mines had sprung up in the region as thousands of avaricious men swarmed into the mountains. A brand new town was rising on the outskirts of old Oro City. The town was so rich and raucous and wicked that everyone who had been there swore Leadville was the wildest town in the West.

Sam Harris brooded as he polished whiskey glasses and emptied spitoons. He had tried to forget his loss and humiliation, but it nagged at him constantly. Late one night, after a long evening of listening to Leadville stories, he made up his mind to go back to California Gulch to see with his own eyes the wealth that should have been his.

He asked his boss for a few days off. In the morning he headed for Leadville. After having heard so many incredible barroom tales about this new boomtown, he thought he was prepared for what he would see when he got there. But what he saw was absolutely astounding.

Leadville's main thoroughfare was lined with tall hotels, saloons, gambling dens, dance halls and bordellos. Ornate variety theaters, featuring both vaudeville acts and boxing matches, stood beside fancy restaurants where patrons walked across floors tiled with silver dollars.

The streets at midday were twice as crowded as Larimer Street on a Saturday night. Hundreds of boisterous men swaggered up and down the wide, slag-paved main avenue amid a continuous parade of freight wagons, coaches and buggies. Every hotel and boarding house was filled to capacity.

When the saloons finally closed at night, men were being allowed to sleep on the floors for a dollar apiece. Others rented tent spaces for 50 cents; the less fortunate slept in packing crates in the alleys.

Sam Harris pushed his way through the bat-wing doors of one of Leadville's most infamous saloons, the Bon Ton. He had seen some tough honky-tonks in his time, but never anything like this one. The high-ceilinged room was packed, almost elbow to elbow, with bellowing, drunken men. The air was blue with cigar smoke and profanity. The clatter of the roulette wheels could scarcely be heard above the din, and the stomping of scores of heavy boots all but drowned out the merry tunes being plinked out by the derby-hatted piano player. Harris soon learned that Leadville's most popular drink was straight whiskey laced with gunpowder, but it wasn't the whiskey that made his head swim. It was the intoxicating stories he listened to as he bellied up to the bar.

"Yes," a bartender told him, "J.F. Matthews is getting very rich, but hell, in Leadville, it seems like everybody's gettin' rich except us bartenders.

"Take that scruffy old ruffian, Horace Tabor. Came to town without a dime in his pockets, hit pay-dirt and now everybody says he's worth about ten million. And then there's James Brown. Nobody knows how much he's worth, but his wife, Molly, wears diamonds bigger'n my pocket watch.

"Yes sir, damn near anybody can get rich overnight in those hills out there. Why, just the other day, old Chicken Bill Fryer died; his relatives dug him a grave behind his cabin and struck silver. Would you like another drink, sir?"

"No thanks," said the dejected Harris. "I'm getting sick to my stomach."

Sam Harris left the Bon Ton and rode out to the Silver Lady Mine. He sat silently in his saddle, gazing up at the enormous mining facilities that had been built on his claim. Seven great wooden towers rose above deep shafts from which mule-drawn ore carts emerged to carry their cargoes to the smelter.

Harris swore under his breath for he knew that every third ingot the Silver Lady produced was rightfully his. He nudged his horse and clopped sullenly back toward Denver. The long, mountain road allowed him plenty of time to think. Soon an idea began to form in his mind. Before long, the idea had grown into a detailed plan. On the day that Harris got back to Larimer Street he was actually smiling.

During the course of his employment as a bartender, Sam Harris had met many men. One of them, a fellow bartender named Cob Lanaghen, had become his closest friend. Lanaghen was a tall, lean, young fellow with steely blue eyes and a fashionable mustache. He had come to Colorado a few years earlier hoping to strike it just rich enough to buy a farm in his native Iowa. Instead he had wound up wiping bar counters on Larimer Street.

When Harris got back to Denver, one of the first things he asked his friend was: "How soon are you going to buy yourself that farm, Cob?"

"Oh hell, Sam," Lanaghen replied. "You know damn well I'll never save up enough money."

"Well now," Harris said with a grin. "Supposing I told you I've got a scheme that'll make us both enough money to buy up half a county of farmland?"

"I'd say you were crazy," Lanaghen laughed. "But go ahead... I'm listening."

Sam Harris proceeded to outline his plan; Cob Lanaghen's eyes widened as the details unfolded. When Harris had finished, Lanaghen said, "You know, Sam, you may not be crazy after all. It just might be you're a genius."

He smoothed his mustache thoughtfully before he said, "You say we'll need two more men. Well, there's certainly plenty of hardcore ruffians right here in this saloon every night. Anyone of them would jump at the chance to join up with us, but how would we know we could trust them?"

"You can't trust anybody nowadays," Harris retorted. "We'll just have to pick the best we can find. And I want them to understand there's to be no gun play. I don't want anyone to get hurt. If all goes well, no one will."

Approximately two weeks later, one of the Silver Lady's regular silver shipments rolled out of Leadville, three heavy wagons pulled by sturdy mules. On each wagon seat, a guard armed with a shotgun and a pistol sat beside the teamster.

The ruggedest, most dangerous part of the trip to Denver was the Park Range trail between Leadville and Berthoud Pass. This narrow, precarious slash across the mountain sides was barely a wagon wide, and it took an extremely skillful muleskinner to maneuver a team up and over this rocky track. The most treacherous section of the trail stretched out above a nearly vertical drop of more than 800 feet. When the wagons reached this point, Sam Harris and Cob Lanaghen stepped out from behind a boulder and pointed double-barreled shotguns at the freighters caught completely off-guard.

"Good morning, gentlemen," Harris said from behind his bandana. "Please set your brakes and give us your undivided attention. We are going to ask a few small favors of you.

"You needn't look over your shoulders, but if you do, you'll see two more members of my gang standing behind you. So the first thing we'd like you to do is throw your firearms over the cliff. For obvious reasons, we don't want any shooting. If just one shot gets fired, your mules will panic and plunge over the edge, taking you and the wagons with them."

Although it was a chilly day, a bead of sweat rolled down the lead driver's face as he glanced at the drop-off just inches from his wagon's wheels. "Do as he says, boys," he gulped, and three shotguns and six pistols clattered down the rocks.

"Thank you," Harris said. "Now get down from the wagons. Be very careful; we don't want anyone to slip and fall. Next we'd like you to unload the first wagon."

After a sizeable pile of silver bars had been stacked on the the ground, Harris said, "That looks like just about enough. Well, gentlemen, here comes the hard part. Unhitch your mules and push the wagons over the edge."

The teamsters stared incredulously at the bandits for a moment; then, they did as they were told. Once the mules were freed of their harnesses, the men put their shoulders to the sides of the wagons and tipped them over, one by one. The falling wagons tumbled down the slope and burst on the rocks in silvery showers of ingots that bounced, leaped, flew and flashed in the sunshine.

"Now everybody step back away from the mules," Harris ordered. He raised his shotgun, aimed it at a cloud and fired both barrels. The terrified animals raced off down the road at break-neck speed, quickly disappearing in the distance.

"Enjoy your walk back to town, boys," said Harris as the grumbling freighters trudged away. When they were all out of sight, the four bandits went at once to a nearby side canyon where they had hidden their horses. They brought the horses back to the stack of ingots and filled their saddle bags with silver bars.

Then they led their over-burdened mounts past the dizzying cliffs to a stretch of trail which crossed a mountain meadow. Here a tall, slim, bearded man waited beside a feed wagon.

The man's name was Grover Edwards, a name well known in the saloons along Larimer Street. It was rumored that Edwards made his living buying and selling stolen goods. One night, Harris had discretely asked him if he would be interested in buying some rather sizable amounts of silver, cash on delivery, of course. Edwards, his eyes aglow, affirmed that he definitely would be interested. With this agreement made, the final part of Harris plan was in place.

Now, out in the high Park Range meadow, Grover Edwards walked, smiling, toward the approaching outlaws. "You boys raised quite a clatter back there," he laughed. "I heard it all the way down here. Well, let's see what you've got here."

As the gang unloaded their saddle bags, Edwards nodded approvingly. "Hide all those bars under the feed sacks in my wagon," he directed. From his coat pocket, he pulled out a big wad of money and began peeling off bills of large denominations. He handed them to Harris, saying, "It was nice doin' business with you boys. I hope I'll see you again soon."

"You will," said Sam Harris.

When J.F. Matthews received news of the silver heist, he grew livid with anger. When the Harris gang struck a second time and a third, Matthews' anger turned to fury. "Who do these crooks think they are?" he thundered. "Do they think they can just rob me with impunity whenever they want? Well, by God, they're going to be in for a little surprise the next time they hit one of my wagons!"

One week later, three Silver Lady wagons rocked and bumped their way over the precipitous Park Range trail. When they reached the section with the steepest drop-off, Harris and Lanaghen stepped out and halted them.

"I'm afraid you bushwhackers are outta luck this time," the lead driver said. "Take a look at our cargoes."

Harris lifted the tarp off the bed of the first wagon and found himself staring at a load of enormous silver bars. "Everyone of them ingots weighs 85 pounds," the driver said, grinning. "Takes two men just to pick one up. So, go ahead... try stuffing one of them in your saddle bag."

Harris dropped the tarp and shrugged this shoulders. "Looks like Mister Matthews has outsmarted us. I guess we'll have to give up our careers as highwaymen. I see no reason to detain your wagons any longer. You are free to go on your way."

Back in Leadville, J.F. Matthews cheered exuberantly when he received word that the shipment had gotten through intact. "From now on," he announced, "all ingots cast in my smelters will weight 85 pounds apiece. This great enterprise will no longer be troubled by two-bit scoundrels!"

The next wagon train to jolt across the treacherous track expected no trouble, so the freighters were more than a little surprised to find Harris and Lanaghen waiting for them. Lanaghen was pointing a shotgun and Harris had a saddlebag draped over his shoulder.

"Aw, fer Christ's sake," the grizzled lead driver groaned. "Ain't you fellas got no common sense? Don't you know you can't steal something you cain't carry away?"

"Oh yes," Harris nodded. "We do know that." He tipped his saddle bag upside down and dumped its contents on the ground. "That's why we brought these saws. Now as soon as you chuck your weapons over the cliff, you can start sawing those ingots in half.

"Mister Matthews is gonna be madder'n Blue Billy Hell when he hears about this," the old muleskinner sputtered as he got down from his wagon seat.

"I certainly hope so," said Harris as he handed the old man a saw.

Predictably Matthews did go through the roof, but after he calmed down he quickly came up with a new idea to thwart the bandits.

When the Harris bunch halted the next shipment, the lead driver grinned and said, "Mister Matthews has got another surprise for you fellas. This time, all these 85-pound ingots were cast with an iron rod through the middle. You can't carry 'em and you cain't saw 'em in half."

"Oh, I don't think that poses much of a problem," Harris replied. "Just saw the ingots lengthwise, right along side of the rods."

Within an hour, several of the silver bars had been cut into manageable sizes. The wagons had been pushed over the cliff and four very pleased bandits rode off toward their rendezvous with Grover Edwards.

Two weeks went by before Harris' gang struck again. This time, when the outlaws appeared in front of the wagon train, the old muleskinner was wearing a smug grin. "You fellows really ought'ta give up," he chuckled. "There ain't no way you can saw these ingots in half without hittin' iron. Each one of them has got a rod cast lengthwise with another cast horizontal. Mister Matthews has got ya this time, ain't he?"

"No," said Harris. "All he's done is make more work for you, oldtimer. I want you boys to just saw a square chuck of silver off each corner of about 20 to 30 of these ingots.

"And if any of you would care to saw off a few souvenirs to stuff in your own coatpockets, I would be the last person to object."

"Well now, sonny," said the old muleskinner, "that's the first worthwhile thing I ever heard you say. Hand me a saw."

Before long, a fair-sized pile of crudely cut silver blocks had been stacked on the ground. "I guess all of you know the next step," Harris said. "Unhitch the mules and tip the wagons over the brink."

The wagoneers released the mules, braced themselves against the side of the first wagon and pushed, sending it tumbling over the escarpment. With a mighty collective heave they toppled the second wagon and moved on to the third.

Then it happened. As the men shoved at the last wagon, a large rock beneath the left front wheel crumbled, fell away and flipped the wagon prematurely over the edge. Everyone jumped back out of the way... everyone except the old muleskinner. Clutching the rim of the wagon bed, he hurtled down the precipice, his mouth open in a silent scream.

As the men on the trail watched in frozen horror, the wagon arched through the air, overturned and exploded on the canyon floor in a burst of shining ingots and flying wagon wheels. The muleskinner slammed spread-eagle into the rocks and lay motionless.

"Oh, my God," said Sam Harris, his voice barely audible behind his bandana. "Oh no. I never wanted anything like this to happen. Oh, Jesus."

"You murderer!" shouted one of the freighters. "You killed that old man the same as if you'd shot him! I hope you hang for this!"

One of the rear-guard bandits ran forward shouting, "C'mon Sam! Let's get the hell outta here!" For one last, long moment, Sam Harris stared down the slope at the crumpled body, then he fled along the trail with his fellow outlaws.

The freighters hurried back to Leadville to report the death and the robbery. When they went to Matthews' office, the president was aghast. "They killed one of the teamsters? This has gone too damned far! Who in the hell are they?"

"I heard one of the bandits call their leader 'Sam,'" one of the freighters said.

"Sam?" Matthews repeated. "That's not much help, is it? But wait a minute. Sam... Sam *Harris!* Yes, that's who it is! It's got to be him!

"You see, Sam Harris was the one who, uh, well, he came to my office once and tried to sell me a phoney claim. I spotted him as a crook right off, and I ordered him out the door. Yes, that's him, all right. That's why he only robs my wagon trains. He's got a grudge against me.

"Well, Mister Sam Harris' days are numbered. I am going to personally put a price on his head so high that every lawman, every bounty hunter, and every would-be gunslinger in the state will be hunting him like a wild animal!"

Within days, wanted posters appeared throughout Lake and Park Counties and beyond. Cob Lanaghen, looking pale and frightened, brought one to the Harris gang's mountain hideout near the tiny town of Redcliff.

"I've already seen it," Harris said glumly when Lanaghen showed the poster. "Our 'partners' came by with one of those flyers about an hour ago. They both took their shares of the loot and lit out for California. I think we better do the same."

Lanaghen agreed: "We don't dare stay around here any longer, that's for sure. But where we gonna run to, Sam? For a ten thousand dollar reward, they'll be trackin' us no matter where we go. They'll never give up. We'll be lookin' over our shoulders for the rest of our lives."

"We'll find a safe place somewhere," Harris vowed.

Lanaghen rubbed his eyes with trembling fingers. "I need time to think," he said. "I'm goin' into Redcliff for a few drinks."

Instantly Harris objected. "That's not a good idea, Cob. They're going to be looking for us even in the smallest towns."

"You're right," Lanaghen conceded. "I'll just buy a bottle and come right back." He left the cabin and rode away.

Sam Harris sat on the edge of his bunk, waiting. Twilight turned into darkness but Cob Lanaghen did not return. Harris paced the floor most of the night, and it was not until noon the next day that Lanaghen walked through the door.

Harris breathed a sign of relief. "You had me worried, pal," he said. "I thought they got you in Redcliff."

Lanaghen hesitated before he spoke. Then he said, "I didn't go to Redcliff, Sam. I went to Leadville."

He paused again before he went on. "I had a talk with J.F. Matthews. He's agreed to drop all charges against me... if I turn you in."

"What?" Harris gasped. "I don't believe what I'm hearing. You're selling me out? You, Cob?"

Lanaghen took a deep breath. "Well, I guess it's like you always said: You can't trust anybody nowadays." He placed his hands on the butt of his pistol. "Don't try to out draw me, Sam. It won't do any good. There's a 20-man posse outside. This cabin's completely surrounded. All you can do is give yourself up."

Harris' face went white, but he unbuckled his gunbelt, let it drop to the floor and walked out with his hands above his head.

Lanaghen watched from the doorway as the lawmen handcuffed his friend and put him on a horse. After the posse had ridden out of sight, he overturned the hearthstone beneath which he and Harris had hidden their money. Once he had stuffed his saddle bags full, he began his long ride back to Iowa. Eventually he purchased a very large piece of land and became a prosperous and highly respected dairy farmer.

J.F. Matthews, of course, went on to become extremely wealthy. He, like the other silver barons of his time, built mansions, developed a taste for opera and cognac and frequently sailed to Europe on luxury liners.

Samuel Bedford Harris was tried and convicted of armed robbery and murder on July 2, 1879. Three days later, he ascended the steps of a newly constructed gallows on Leadville's Chestnut Avenue. He stood expressionless on the trapdoor while leather straps were wrapped and tightened around his ankles, thighs and arms. He stared straight ahead, knowing that the one person he could trust to do exactly what he expected was the hangman.

Bibliography - Chapter 8

Ballenger, Dean. *Westerner* magazine. Encino, California. Behn-Miller Publications. January -February, 1973.

Burgos, Carl. *Great West* magazine. New York. N.F. Enterprises, Inc. June 1974.

Dallas, Sandra. **Colorado Ghost Towns and Mining Camps.** Norman, Oklahoma. University of Oklahoma Press. 1985.

Hill, Alice Polk. **Tales of the Colorado Pioneers.** Glorieta, New Mexico. The Rio Grande Press, Inc. 1976 reprint.

9

Treasures Lost & Found

In a state as mineral rich as Colorado, it is no surprise to learn that treasure stories abound...lost mines and buried strongboxes, long-forgotten false graves with coffins full of priceless coins, hidden caves where grinning skulls guard stacks of gold bars. Such tales are as varied as the mountains themselves.

Colorado's legendary treasure stories date back to the early Spanish explorations. According to some accounts, Fray Silvestre Vélez de Escalante discovered both gold and silver in 1776 in southwestern Colorado, somewhere near contemporary Cortez. One hundred years later, two U.S. Cavalry officers, Merrick and Mitchell, discovered the crumbled ruins of a crude forge along with a scattering of rich gold and silver nuggets.

Since Escalante brought out little or no gold when he completed his explorations, it has always been assumed that he buried a small fortune and left it to await his return. If so, it is waiting still; after another one hundred years of searching, only a few roughly chiseled crosses and semi-circles have been found on boulders and long-dead trees.

In 1790, a French expedition led by a man named Lebreau is said to have crossed over Wolf Creek Pass and traveled south into the San Juan Mountains where they discovered and mined considerable amounts of gold. A brutal winter took the lives of many of these intrepid men. When spring finally came, the survivors, sick and half-starved, cached their treasure in the mine shaft.

Lebreau drew up a detailed map on a piece of oiled silk upon which he carefully marked the locations of the directional rock cairns he had stacked along the trailless route between his mine and Wolf Creek Pass. He returned to France in 1792. In his old age, he passed his map on to his grandson.

Lebreau's grandson traveled to Colorado in 1844, determined to locate the treasure. Unfortunately, he was drowned trying to cross the San Juan River. His body was recovered, but the map was lost forever.

At this late date, it is improbable that anyone will ever determine whether or not these and other pre-territorial treasure tales are true stories or fables. If these mythic riches actually exist, they are undoubtedly forever unrecoverable. But enough of Colorado's lost treasure *has* been found to keep all the legends alive.

A fascinating example is the story of the Lost Ute Gold, or, as it was sometimes called, The Lost Chimney Rock Treasure.

This little drama began in the autumn of either 1851 or 1852, when a party of five white men on horseback led five heavily loaded pack mules along a trail now known as Highway 160 between Durango and Pagosa Springs. Each mule carried two large sacks of gold bullion, very likely the loot from a rather sizeable robbery.

As the men rode through the piñon forests not far from the great jagged landmark, Chimney Rock, they suddenly came upon a small Ute encampment. There were no Indian men in the camp; just a dozen or more women and many children. The Indians reacted in terrified surprise at the appearance of these fierce looking strangers.

It is possible that these Utes had never seen white men before, but even more likely that they had never seen men as beastly as these. The intruders, slouching in their saddles, had long, shaggy hair and big, black, bushy beards. To the women and children, they looked like men with the heads of buffalos. They ran screaming into the trees to hide.

The darkly whiskered men studied the emptied camp and saw deer meat hanging on a drying rack. They dismounted and helped themselves. Then as they swung back on their horses, a slight mishap occurred. When one of the men hefted himself into his saddle, his horse shied sideways, bumped a teepee, knocking it down.

The incident seemed so trivial that the jerky-chewing riders scarcely bothered to glance back before they clopped away, completely unaware that their clumsiness had sealed their fates.

A small campfire inside the toppled teepee burst into flames. In no time the dry grass in the encampment caught fire and the blaze swept into two more teepees. By the time the women were able to beat out the fires with blankets, half the camp had gone up in smoke.

The stunned, trembling women were standing in the smoldering ashes when the Ute males returned from their hunting trip. The agitated women graphically described the fearsome, bestial men who had senselessly destroyed their camp. The eyes of a young Ute chieftain narrowed; his mouth tightened into a hard, thin line. "Those were not men," he told the other braves. "They are demons. They must be killed or they will return to cause even greater harm."

The warriors agreed. They took up their weapons and moved off swiftly on the trail of the white men. By night fall, the war party had reached a high ridge not far from Chimney Rock. The black sky above them was filled with a million stars, but in the dark hills rolling out ahead of them, only one flickering pinpoint of light was visible. The Utes moved on soundlessly toward the distant campfire.

Stealthily, they encircled the sleeping men and settled down to wait for dawn. When the first rays of light pushed away the darkness, the Utes rose from their hiding place and fired a lightning-fast shower of arrows into the still-slumbering, blanketed figures.

One of the five men had risen early and was urinating in the bushes when he heard the screams of his dying comrades. He fled headlong into the trees, trashed wildly through the brush to escape.

The warriors did not bother to pursue him, perhaps knowing he was too terrified to ever return. They gathered up the dead men's blankets and firearms, rounded up their horses and mules and took them as partial payment for the damage done to their homes.

The Utes had no use for the gold bullion they found, so they threw it in a shallow ravine nearby. Since there were virtually no white settlers in the area at the time, no one but the Utes knew about the massacre for many years. Finally, in about 1890, an old man drifted into Archuleta County. His name was Slim

Carven, a former outlaw who had spent most of the latter part of his life in prison. He told the local folks he had traveled through the San Juan country nearly 40 years earlier with a pack train that had been ambushed by Indians. His companions had all been slain, he said, and the gold they were carrying had been stolen. He had always felt sure the Indians would have hidden the gold nearby. So now at last, he had come back to search for it.

Upon hearing Carven's story, nearly everyone in the county came down with a bad case of gold fever. Several prominent citizens accompanied Carven to the Indian agency on the Southern Ute Reservation where they talked to an ancient man who spent most of his time dozing in the sunshine alongside the plank-board walls of the trading post. This elderly Ute was known locally as "Old Washington." No one knew his age, but everyone agreed his memory was still absolutely phenomenal.

Old Washington listened to Slim Carven's story. Finally, he said yes, he remembered hearing that several devilish men had once been slain near Chimney Rock. Their gold had been dumped in a shallow ravine not far from the dead men's camp, he related.

That was enough to unleash a massive search. Throughout the summer, scores of men tromped the hills digging and probing the earth. They found nothing. Four decades of mountain rains and snow-melt had buried the cache under dirt and gravel. The disappointed Carven wandered away. The locals gave up as well.

Six years later, in 1896, a young Indian and his wife entered the office at the Durango smelter. From beneath his red and white striped blanket, the Ute drew out a bright gold bar about one inch square and six inches long. He showed it to the assayer, Dick Keller, and offered to sell it.

Keller excitedly bombarded the Indian with questions. Where had he found this gold? Was there more where this came from? Could he lead others to the spot? The Ute promptly grew very suspicious. He put the gold bar back under his blanket and walked out the door never to return.

When the folks around Durango heard about Keller's visitor, they were all quite certain that the unknown Indian had discovered the long-lost Chimney Rock Treasure. But no one knew who he was, nor what the Ute might have done with the gold bar. Local whites watched carefully for any signs of sudden wealth among the Utes, but there was no evidence of that. Perhaps the young Indian was so fearful that the gold would be taken from him that he simply re-hid it.

In 1955, a Colorado history buff, Temple H. Cornelius, wrote to the *Durango News* to comment on the passing of an old Ute friend of his. He noted, "Page Wright was a real old-timer in the San Juan. He convinced me that he was actually the one who found the Chimney Rock Treasure, but, though I pressed him for further information, he would never reveal the exact location of his find, nor the way in which he disposed of it."

That remembrance of old Page Wright is the last word so far on this particular treasure story, so its final ending is still a mystery. But it is not the only tale of Colorado Indians discovering gold.

An old black man, Henry Jackson, had lived most of his life in a log cabin near Devil's Head Mountain in the Rampart Range. Since he was a friendly, hospitable fellow, he always got along well with the Utes living in the area. Jackson remembered that during the 1870s, groups of Indians frequently rode by his home on their way into the network of gulches and gullies spreading out around Jarre Canyon, close to Devil's Head. The Utes would return a few days later laden down with heavy buckskin bags of ore.

On his visits to the Ute village, Jackson had observed the Indian women crushing the ore with stones and washing it in a trough made of a hollowed out log. After the pulverized sand had been sifted away, the tiny particles of gold were gathered up and put in the quills of wild goose feathers. The golden quills were taken to the nearest trading post where they were exchanged for blankets, whiskey and ammunition.

This primitive style of mining and trading apparently continued sporadically until 1881 when the Utes were forcibly removed from the area. In 1900 or thereabouts, two wandering prospectors stopped by Henry Jackson's lonely cabin. Naturally, Jackson invited them in. He dished up some beans and hot coffee and spent the evening regaling them with tales about the old days.

The prospectors were enthralled by the story of the Utes' gold. They promptly decided to go in search of the mine. Jackson did not see them again throughout the summer, but when they passed by his cabin again in the early fall, they were two very happy men.

The prospectors told Jackson they had found the Ute mine, and it was a very rich vein of gold-bearing quartz. They had already dug out and panned a considerable amount of gold which they now planned to sell in Denver. "See you next spring, Henry," they shouted as they led their donkeys away.

Spring never came for those two exuberant young men; Henry Jackson learned later they they had been ambushed by bandits who took both their lives and their gold.

One year later, a brother of one of the prospectors arrived at Jackson's doorstep to ask the old man if he knew where his brother's mine was located. Jackson admitted he had no idea where it might be. He declined the young man's offer to join him in searching for it.

"I'm too old to go trampin' around the hills," Jackson said. "But I wish you the best of luck."

Several weeks went by before the brother returned with a look of defeat in his eyes. He said he found the place where the miners had hidden their tools, but he never found any sign of a mine or mine tailings.

Henry Jackson shook his head sympathetically. "That shore is a shame. But it ain't at all surprisin.' Them young fellers was too smart to stash their tools anywheres near their diggin's. And most likely they done shoveled their tailin's back into their tunnel and covered it over 'fore they left. I expect that mine is just plain lost forever."

That did appear to be the case. Even though many others searched the area during the next decade, no one found the murdered men's mine. Then in 1911, a man named Carl R. Johnson hiked up one of Jarre Canyon's brushy gullies to hunt rabbits. With his shotgun in hand, he pushed his way through the dense, thorny underbrush. As he moved along, he noticed that the gully's rocky slopes contained several visible veins of rose quartz. From each of these veins, he chipped out a chunk of rock and carried them all out in his rucksack.

Later, he crushed and panned the crystals. All of his samples were worthless but one which yielded a promising string of colors. Johnson was pretty sure he knew where he had picked it up. While he had walked along, he had seen a rabbit hop into a clump of bushes.

He shot at it, then discovered a small tunnel when he went over to find his prey. It was there that he had found the richest nugget. As soon as possible, Johnson hurried back to the gully. He spent days wading and crawling through clump after clump of scraggly brush but never relocated the tunnel. And apparently even to this day, no one else has either.

One of Colorado's most poignant treasure stories is the romantic legend of the Lost Arapaho Princess Treasure. This tale may only be folkloric, since no one can prove it is true. Still, enough people have believed it to have spent years looking for the treasure.

This story begins on an unspecified date in the 1770s, when a small Spanish expedition explored a mountain range in southern Colorado known today as the Spanish Peaks. The Spaniards struck gold somewhere high in the foothills and set up a mining operation. Several bands of Arapahos lived in these foothills, so as the mine grew larger, the Spanish hired a number of Indians to help.

The leader of the expedition must have been a rather exceptional man. Unlike most Spanish explorers, he was neither cruel nor arrogant; he was handsome but not vain, intense yet sensitive. He respected the Arapaho people and they, in turn, grew to respect him.

The chief of the Arapahos is said to have had a beautiful daughter, a lovely woman whose eyes were dark as night and whose smile was as bright as dawn. The "princess" and the ardent young Spaniard fell in love; with her father's blessing, they were married. Within a year, the Arapaho bride gave birth to a baby girl, fulfilling the young couple's happiness.

By now the Spaniards had mined a substantial amount of gold. It was time to return to Santa Fe. The expedition leader ordered half of the gold buried in a secret spot not far from a prominent rock formation which he named *La Muñeca*, since, from a certain angle it resembled a giant doll. To mark the exact spot of the carefully hidden treasure, he wedged a shovel into a vertical crack in a large boulder.

After the rest of the gold and enough provisions for the journey were loaded onto a small caravan of pack animals, the new father bid goodbye to his beloved wife and newborn daughter. He vowed to return within a month.

The trail to Santa Fe was slow and arduous in those days, but the stalwart Spaniards reached the dusty City of Holy Faith without mishap. Here they were surprised to learn they were being sent on to the *presidio* of San Miguel de Orcasitas to join Don Juan Bautista de Anza's expedition into the Colorado River country. They would be gone for at least two years.

The young father could not bear the thought of being separated from his family, so he gave up his command, resigned his officer's commission and rode back to the Spanish Peaks alone.

When he arrived in the Arapaho village he found everyone in mourning. His wife was dead; she had been bitten by a timber rattler while gathering firewood.

The stunned husband's sorrow was so great that he unsheathed his dagger, poised its blade over his heart and prepared to join his wife. Then he let the knife fall, realizing that he had to live to raise his infant daughter.

The grieving man came to believe that, somehow, the gold had caused his tragedy. He was convinced there was a curse on the treasure and never went near it again.

The Spaniard's daughter grew up to be a beautiful woman just like her mother. On the day she married a brave Arapaho warrior, her aging father at last told her about the curse. "Never go near *La Muñeca*," he ordered. "Never let your husband or the children you will bear dig beneath the rock marked with a shovel."

The daughter heeded her father's warning and kept the location secret until she, herself, was very old. Finally as she neared her last days, she passed the story on to her eldest son.

The son, however, did not believe in curses. Shortly after his mother died, he went in search of the gold. He soon located the marked rock, beneath which he noticed a small hole in the ground. He pried the rusty shovel out of the rock and used it to enlarge the opening. Then, bending down on his knees, he reached deep inside the dark hole, groping eagerly with both hands —into a seething den of rattlesnakes.

Screams of the Spanish explorer's grandson echoed across the foothills as he ran wildly down the slope, waving his poisoned arms until he fell dead. He was the last person to ever know the exact location of the Lost Arapaho Princess Treasure. No one has been able to find it. It may be better that way.

Out of all of Colorado's scores of treasure stories, surely the strangest and eeriest are the ones about great fortunes allegedly hidden in caves. Three of these tales became fairly famous. One of them cannot be proven nor disproved; the other two have been verified. The existence of those two caves is firmly established. Even though they have been explored, they are still shrouded in mysteries as dark as their subterranean depths.

The story of the as-yet-to-be-rediscovered "lost cave" was told by S.J. Harkman, E.R. Oliver and H.A. Melton in 1860. In October of that year, these three prospectors were caught in a sudden, unseasonably furious blizzard in the Sangre de Cristo Mountains in Saguache County. They staggered blindly through the swirling snow knowing they would perish if they did not find shelter before nightfall.

Certainly they would have all frozen to death had it not been for a fortuitous accident. One of the three desperate men fell into a hole as he groped his way along the side of a steep, rocky slope.

The hole, he quickly discovered, was the entrance of a narrow, horizontal cave. The men crawled single-file through the tunnel until they reached a large chamber in which they could stand upright. This room was damp and cold, and darker than the darkest night.

Melton crawled back out and braved the storm again long enough to gather firewood. The wood was wet, of course, but he used the old frontiersman's method for obtaining dry tinder. He turned over a large log and scooped up the dry pine needles and twigs from beneath it.

Once the prospectors got a smoldering fire going inside the cave, they warmed themselves as they glanced about the shadowy underground room. Harkman gasped audibly and jumped up. Beside his boot was a human skull.

The three men lifted the burning pine branch from their fire and explored the smokey cavern. Along one wall, they found four more skulls and a pile of skeletons. On the opposite side of the chamber, the flickering torches revealed a lengthy stack of what at first appeared to be thick, flat stones. On closer examination, they proved to be solid gold bars.

It seems safe to assume the astonished trio slept a bit restlessly that night, surrounded by a moldy tangle of skeletons and a fortune in gold while a blizzard howled wildly outside the cave. By morning, the storm had blown itself out. Melton, Oliver and Harkman packed up as much gold as they could carry away and headed for Saguache.

There they wintered comfortably, waiting for the high country snows to melt before they went back for the rest of the gold. But, as so often happens, when they tried to retrace the route of their frantic flight out of the mountains, they could not even relocate the right canyon.

All through the summer of 1881, Melton, Oliver and Harkman scrambled around the valleys and slopes searching in vain. They eventually concluded that the cave's small mouth had been covered over by a spring-time landslide. If so, the skeletons and the gold bars are forever entombed in the Lost Cave of the Skulls.

The 40-year search for the Lost Reynolds Gang's Loot had a very different ending.

This bloody little drama began when five infamous outlaws, hot out of Texas, thundered into the Fairplay area in 1864. These murderous thieves had been plundering and robbing small towns, ranches and innocent travelers across West Texas for the previous three years. Now with half the lawmen west of Abilene on their trail, they decided it might be in their best interest to high-tail it out of Texas for a little fresh, high-country air in Colorado.

Two reckless brothers were leaders of this ruth-less bunch, John and James Reynolds. For their first Colorado caper, the Reynolds Gang chose to rob the Fairplay-to-Denver stagecoach. It proved to be an easy heist; they galloped off with an estimated $60,000 in gold dust and cash.

They hit the stagecoach at Kenosha Pass on the South Park stage road, a mere 20 miles from Denver. As soon as word of the crime reached the city, David Cook, chief of government detectives, dispatched a large posse into the area. The lawmen spotted the gang's camp high in the southern foothills of Mount Logan and converged upon it.

The outlaws were just packing up to move on when the forest around them billowed blue with gunsmoke. The posse's first withering barrage cut down everyone but the two Reynolds brothers. James Reynolds tried to shoot his way out of the encirclement, but when he realized he didn't have a chance, he threw down his pistols and surrendered.

John Reynolds was luckier. He grabbed the saddlebags containing the loot, slung himself on his horse and made a desperate dash through the trees. The outlaw lost the posse near the headwaters of Deer Creek. Here he found a small cave into which he stashed the gold after stuffing his pockets with cash. He covered the cave entrance with rocks before leaving. He rode to Santa Fe to cool his heels awhile. Before long, he teamed up with a local desperado named Albert Brown. As partners, the two bandits pulled off a few small-time robberies in northern New Mexico.

But these robberies were hardly worth the risk to John Reynolds, since he knew he had a fair-sized fortune waiting for him in a shallow Colorado cave. He decided it was time to sneak back into Colorado to retrieve his treasure. The two bandits might well have succeeded had they not made a fatal mistake along the way.

Somewhere north of Taos, they made a sidetrip to an isolated ranch to steal fresh horses. To their surprise, the ranch hands fought them furiously. John Reynolds caught a load of buckshot in his stomach. He managed to stay on his horse for a few miles, then he fell to the ground.

Before he died, he tried to draw a treasure map for his partner. Legend has it that since he had no pencil, Reynolds asked Brown to sharpen a bullet which he used to smear lines on a piece of cigaret paper. At least he finished before his eyes glazed over and the bullet fell from his hand.

Albert Brown headed on to Colorado and the slopes of Mount Logan. It didn't take him long to realize the map was sorely inadequate. Though he searched the area between Deer Creek and Geneva gulch over and over, he never did find the carefully concealed entrance. But he was certain he came close.

None of the other searchers found it during their long, arduous efforts in the next 30 years. The cave remained lost until April 28, 1906. The *Rocky Mountain News* reported that two treasure hunters named Sullivan Davis and Holmes Robbins had rediscovered it and that it contained $18,000 in gold dust.

This is a puzzling sum since the original robbery was said to have netted at least $60,000. What became of the rest of the treasure? Did Reynolds lose some of it as he fled? Or did he hide the gold in two different locations? Whatever the answer, there is a strong possibility that a substantial portion of the Lost Reynolds Gang's Loot is still out there somewhere near the base of Mount Logan.

The most mysterious Colorado cave is the one called *La Caverna del Oro*. It is also the most difficult and dangerous to enter. This near-vertical shaft, located at the 11,550-foot level of Marble Mountain southwest of Westcliffe is over 300 feet deep. In winter, half its depth fills with snow. During the rest of the year, its humidity is above 95 percent. Temperature in the cave is never above 34 degrees. Cold, violent subterranean winds often roar out of the cave's mouth. In the days when the Indians still lived in the area, it is said the children used to wrap a rock in a blanket, throw it in and then watch as the blanket came flying back out.

The legend of *La Caverna del Oro* goes back more than 200 years.

Supposedly a small contingent of Spanish soldiers arrived in the region in the late 18th century searching for gold. Near Marble Mountain they found a few flakes in the stream. They assumed the source to be higher up, so they explored the mountain's slopes where they found the cave.

Their descent into its gloomy depths must have been quite perilous, for they used wooden ladders and had only pine torches for light. But they did discover gold and mined it with forced Indian labor.

There are two versions of what finally became of these Spaniards. One tale has it that the Indians rebelled and slew their cruel masters; the other says the Spaniards eventually loaded up their gold and traveled on.

One hundred years passed. In 1869, an elderly Hispanic woman told the legend to U.S. Army Captain Elisha P. Horn. The entrance of the cave, she said, was marked by a strange, black cross painted on a boulder. This cross resembled four arrowheads with their points touching. Captain Horn located the marker —which he recognized as a Maltese cross— and found the cave. He wisely did not venture far inside.

The following year, J.H. Yeoman and a group of explorers lowered themselves nearly 200 feet into the cavern where they found several rotted ladders and an ancient hand-cranked windlass. It was not until 1932, however, that the most startling discovery was made.

Four cavers from Denver descended 225 feet into

the widest part of the cave where they came across a manacled skeleton. According to the *Rocky Mountain News*, "With a metal strap encircling the neck, the pile of bones reclined against the rock wall as if the person who died there had been chained in a sitting position and left to starve."

The next serious attempt to go deeper into this haunted, seemingly bottomless abyss was not made until 1952 when an intrepid Colorado spelunker, John Streich, led a well-equipped, three-man team down to the 300-foot level. "We found vast quantities of crumbling rope and numerous passageways that led in all directions," he later wrote.

Streich returned to *La Caverna del Oro* in 1957. At last he reached a depth of 350 feet where the cave veers off into a horizontal crawl way. "We crept along it for 150 feet to its head where we found two waterfalls and pools," he wrote. "Not wanting to get soaked, we stopped at this point."

Since then, this treacherous pit has been fairly well mapped, but no evidence of gold diggings has been verified. Its mysterious past remains unrevealed. Its full story, like all of Colorado's other fabled treasure tales, has no final ending.

How to Follow Colorado's Lost Treasure Trails

All contemporary treasure hunters, whether professional or amateur, will agree that a searcher's most essential tool is a transmit-receive metal detector. But obviously metal detectors are of no help if they are not scanning the right place. Locational clues are needed... the kinds that a very observant off-trail hiker can find.

Rock cairns placed to lead from one point to another can be located even now, but they are usually difficult to see in the underbrush that has grown up around them over the years.

Symbols carved on trees or chiseled on rocks were also used to mark the way back to hidden riches. Horizontal arrows, daggers or snakes point the way toward the treasures and are sometimes accompanied by rough depictions of landscape features. For example, a convex semi-circle with a dot below it indicates the spot on a nearby mountain where gold was buried or a mine was sealed.

Directional changes along the route may appear as a vertical line with a diagonal slash to the left or right; a tilted "D" was a way of saying, "Go downhill."

Exact sites were marked in a variety of ways; downward pointing arrows, crosses, stars or simply an "X." Often, knives were driven into trees at such an angle that the handle pointed directly at the treasure.

Everyone who left these markers believed he would follow them back someday to retrieve a hidden fortune. Some of them did, of course, and in other cases, later searchers have recovered the treasure once considered lost forever.

Therein lies the problem, even if you successfully follow a treasure trail, someone else may have been there ahead of you.

Bibliography - Chapter 9

Baier, Edward. *True Treasure* magazine. Conroe, Texas. True Treasure Publications, Inc. November-December, 1974.

Bancroft, Caroline and Nafziger, Anges. **Colorado's Lost Mines and Buried Treasure.** Boulder, Colorado. Johnson Publishing Company. 1961.

Christopher, Gary W. *Treasure World* magazine. Conroe,

Texas. Treasure World Publications, Inc. October-November, 1974.

Dickerson, Beverly. *True Treasure* magazine. Conroe, Texas. True Treasure Publications, Inc. January-February, 1974.

Erberich, Gerry. *Treasure World* magazine. Conroe, Texas. Treasure World Publishing Company, Inc. October-November, 1975.

Kildare, Maurice. *Frontier Times* magazine. Austin, Texas. December-January, 1971.

Marshall, John B. and Cornelius, Temple H. **Golden Treasures of the San Juan.** Denver. Sage Books. 1961.

Spencer, P.J. *Treasure World* magazine. Conroe, Texas. Treasure World Publishing Company, Inc. October-November, 1975.

10

A Search for the Origins
of UFOs

Of all the mysteries that have perplexed the oft-bewildered people on planet Earth, few have been more fascinating, more frustrating, or had more profound implications than the eternal riddle of unidentified flying objects.

From biblical times to the present, from Ezekiel's fiery wheel in the sky to the flying saucers of today, earthlings have tried in vain to explain or dismiss the

strange aerial phenomenon that persistently appear
above this small world in a variety of forms, shapes
and illuminations. Sometimes they flash, sometimes
hover, and often glow... but always they disappear far
too quickly.

In the years immediately following World War II,
the reported sightings of UFOs increased dramatically
worldwide. Thousands of UFOs were detected by radar
or observed by professional pilots, police officers, mete-
orologists and astronomers as well as by startled members of the general public. Some people have claimed to
have been abducted by aliens aboard strange space
craft, and others say they are in constant communication with other-worldly beings.

Although the more outlandish claims were gener-
ally discredited by authorities, the accumulation of
apparently authenticated reports was sufficient to
warrant an official investigation of the phenomenon by
the early 1950s.

In 1951, the United States Air Force was concerned enough to launch a probe called "Project Blue
Book". The investigation over a 15-year period attempted to evaluate more than 10,000 reported UFO sightings. Several thousands of these were easily dismissed
as the misidentification of natural phenomena or of
man-made objects such as weather balloons, and a
number of hoaxes were uncovered.

Still, far too many cases that defied easy explanation were simply labeled "possible balloon" or "possible aircraft." Critics of the Project Blue Book final
report alleged the military had drawn a "brass curtain"
around the effort so that physical evidence was hidden,
facts were twisted and statistics were misused.

Even so, 646 UFO cases were eventually classified as "unidentified' or "unknown." This astonishing

number by itself made it clear that further scientific study was needed.

The Air Force's Scientific Advisory Board agreed and recommended that a contract be let with at least one leading university to conduct a "prompt and in depth" investigation of UFO sightings. Consequently on October 6, 1966, the Air Force announced it had signed a $313,000, 15-month contract with the University of Colorado to carry out a comprehensive study of "the UFO problem."

Immediately, the little known college town of Boulder, Colorado became the focus of national attention. Here in the eastern foothills of the Rocky Mountains, a serious attempt was about to be made to solve one of the world's greatest mysteries. Perhaps, at last, the inexplicable would be explained.

But how? How could a phenomenon which suddenly and unexpectedly appears and quickly vanishes be studied scientifically? Obviously if the University of Colorado UFO project was to have even the slightest chance of success, it would need expertise from many fields of inquiry. The Air Force appropriation authorized the hiring of a staff of psychologists, an astrogeophysicist, and a psychometrician. This staff would, in turn, retain the consulting services of specialists in nuclear and solar physics, meteorology, physical chemistry, electrical engineering, photographic analysis, radar anomalies, optics and psychiatry.

Private UFO research organizations such as the National Investigations Committee on Aerial Phenomena (NICAP) and the Aerial Phenomena Research Organization (APRO), realizing this investigation would make or break the future of government funded UFO research, offered to assist the project. The Air Force was fully aware that the general public would be highly suspicious of any UFO study sponsored by the military unless it could be shown from the start that this time the study was to be truly objective. To prove the project would be independent, the Air Force chose a staunchly individualistic man to serve as its director.

Dr. Edward Uhler Condon was a professor in the University of Colorado Department of Physics and Astrophysics. Prior to that he had acted as a special advisor to the Senate Committee on Atomic Energy. His fiercely independent nature and his keen mind made him appear to be the perfect person to head the Colorado UFO project. As it turned out, he was absolutely the worst possible choice because what he lacked was essential: an open mind.

Members of Condon's staff were eager to get the project under way, but first they spent hours debating what the primary focus of the study should be. They faced an unprecedented opportunity to learn more about various natural aerial phenomena but, since the general public's principal concern, and fear, was that UFOs come from outer space, the Condon Committee finally decided to concentrate on an attempt to prove or disprove the extraterrestrial origins of UFOs.

An "extraterrestrial intelligence hypothesis" was developed, acknowledging the possibility that at least some UFOs were from a world other than this one. The committee carefully complied a "case book" composed of approximately 100 well-documented sightings, both historic and current, which seemed creditable enough to study.

Dr. David R. Saunders, the team's psychometrician, came up with an intriguing idea. He pointed out that if the committee could discover just one absolutely airtight case of an extraterrestrial incursion, it would be worth more than a dozen almost perfect cases. All it would take, he said, was to establish irrefutably that the planet Earth had actually been visited just once from outer space to prove the "extraterrestrial intelligence hypothesis" was valid. If two or more such cases could be developed, the hypothesis could not possibly be ignored. Further scientific study would be mandated. One case that seemed especially promising was a 1950 sighting which had been filmed. Saunders thought it was imperative that the committee view and analyze this short strip of 16-millimeter film which was commonly referred to as the "Montana UFO Movie."

In Great Falls, Montana, on August 15, 1950, Nick Mariana, the manager of the local baseball team, was checking the wind direction in the ballpark in preparation for the afternoon game when he glanced up and saw two silvery discs silently and rapidly crossing the sky. He shouted at his secretary, Virginia Raunig, to come out of her office as he ran to his car and grabbed his movie camera.

Nick Mariana was able to film the objects for 16 seconds during which time they passed behind a water tower and a grain elevator before going out of sight. "Miss Raunig and I stood there spellbound," he said later. "Suddenly, directly behind us, two jets shot by and we almost jumped out of our shoes."

Mariana rushed his film off to be processed. When it came back, he showed it repeatedly to friends and civic organizations. Everyone who viewed the footage agreed a flying saucer had at last been captured on film.

On October 4, 1950, the Air Force Office of Special Investigations asked Mariana to loan his film to them for examination. He complied, somewhat reluctantly. Weeks later, the Air Force announced that enlargements of several frames did reveal two bright objects streaking across the sky, but photoanalysis proved the objects were just two sun-reflecting F-94 jets which landed at Great Falls Air Force Base a few minutes earlier.

This explanation was too flimsy to be taken seriously. The jets did not make their appearance until after the the UFOs appeared; they had flown in from the northeast, not the northwest as the UFOs had done. Mariana was pointing his camera in the opposite direction from the jets' flight paths. The jets did not pass behind the grain elevator or the water tower.

Saunders and the entire Colorado UFO Project staff viewed the Mariana film in the spring of 1967. Saunders came away believing he had found a perfect case. He felt sure it would not be the only one.

Another promising case was one that had occurred off the coast of Brazil near Ubatuba in September 1957. Several fishermen had sighted a large flying disc zooming toward the beach at a tremendous speed. It appeared about to crash into the sea when it suddenly shot straight up and exploded in mid-air.

Thousands of fiery fragments fell like a huge display of fireworks into the water. Several landed on the shore and were picked up by the fishermen. These small objects were of a thin, grey metallic material much lighter than aluminum. Those fragments were later taken to the Mineral Production Laboratory of the Brazilian Ministry of Agriculture where they were subjected to chemical and spectrographic analysis. The tests showed the metal to be unusually pure magnesium with traces of magnesium hydroxide.

According to Dr. Olavo Fontes, APRO's special representative for Brazil; "The samples represent something outside the range of present-day technological development in earth science. They are, in fact, fragments of an extraterrestrial vehicle which met with disaster in the earth's atmosphere."

Fontes sent three of the fragments to APRO headquarters in Tucson, Arizona, where they were locked away in a safety deposit box. APRO allowed the Condon Committee to borrow one fragment to be examined by a new and highly sophisticated scientific technique known as neutron activation analysis. This complex process, using a gamma ray spectrometer, measures all the mineral elements in a sample up to amounts as small as one part in a million.

The test, conducted by the Federal Bureau of Investigation in Washington, DC, determined the tiny fingernail-size particle to be 99.9 percent magnesium. If the sample had been a terrestrial magnesium alloy, it would have contained aluminum, copper and calcium, but it did not. The technology to purify magnesium to this degree did not exist on planet Earth in 1957. The "extraterrestrial intelligence hypothesis" was looking more and more viable.

Most of the older cases the committee reopened did not yield this sort of incontestable evidence. There were plenty of radar-confirmed sightings, reliable eye witness accounts and scores of photographs to be studied, but it was nearly impossible to add any new information to the old. Current cases offered much better opportunities for investigation.

The Condon Committee had set up an "early warning system" through which it would immediately be notified of new sightings around the country. As Saunders had predicted, there were scores of them. Many sightings were quite ordinary and no different than thousands of earlier ones... mainly just weird lights in the sky or unexplainable blips on radar screens. But two reports were so exceptionally strange that they became "classic" cases in the annals of UFOl-ogy.

The first occurred in Manitoba, Canada on the afternoon of May 20, 1967. Steven Michalak, a Win-nipeg mechanic, was pursuing his hobby of amateur prospecting. That weekend, he had gone alone to a secluded, rough and rocky area near Falcon Lake. He was examining a vein of quartz when a flock of Canadi-an geese flew off the surface of the lake, cackling in alarm.

Curious, Michalak stepped out in the open and saw two glowing oval-shaped UFOs hovering in the air. Within seconds, one sped away and the other descend-ed to the ground. "It just sat there," Michalak recalled. "For 30 minutes, it radiated heat and changed color, from red to a stainless steel grey." Then a door on the side slid open and a brilliant purple light poured out along with the pungent smell of sulphur.

Michalak could hear voices coming from inside, but he could not understand what was being said. Cautiously, he moved to within touching distance of the disc and peered inside. The interior was a maze of flashing lights. He stepped closer, placing his hand on the seamless hull as he leaned forward. Instantly his rubberized glove melted and his shirt burst into flames.

Frantically, Michalak tore off the burning shirt, threw it away and ran madly back to the highway where he flagged down a passing motorist. He was taken to Misericordia Hospital where he was treated for burns on his chest and then released. Later he report-ed his experience to the Royal Canadian Mounted Police and the news media.

In the days that followed, Michalak became very ill. He could not keep food in his stomach; he felt dizzy and nauseated. He suffered a weight loss of 22 pounds. Blisters and a painful red rash appeared on his burned skin. Michalak was treated by a radiologist and a dermatologist, but five months passed before he fully recovered his health.

When the Colorado UFO Project learned about the Falcon Lake landing, a field investigator was sent to Winnipeg. Roy Craig, a physical chemist, interviewed Michalak at length and hiked with him to the lake shore site on the Manitoba-Ontario line. To their surprise, they found the outline of the craft was still plainly visible on the ground. The branches of the trees around the imprint were withered and dead, while trees further away flourished normally. They found the remains of the burnt shirt along with a tape measure Michalak had lost that day. Craig photographed the site, picked up rock and soil samples and flew back to Boulder.

The next classic case to come to the committee's attention took place near Ashland, Nebraska on December 3, 1967. At 2:30 a.m. a local police patrolman, Herbert Schirmer, was driving toward the intersection of Highways 6 and 63 on the outskirts of town. About a quarter of a mile ahead, he sighted a series of red, blinking lights near the ground. When he drove closer he saw that the lights were flashing from oval portholes in a landed, football-shaped UFO. The object had a polished, metal exterior, a catwalk around its periphery, and it was balanced on tripod legs. As the police officer watched through his windshield, the craft shot upward, emitting a siren-like noise and a red-orange flame from its underside before vanishing in the sky.

The sighting seemed to last no more than two or three minutes, but when Schirmer looked at his watch, it was nearly 3 a.m. More than 20 minutes had elapsed, yet he had no memory of them. He drove quickly to the police station and made an entry in his logbook which began: "Saw a FLYING SAUCER! Believe it or not!"

When news of the Ashland incident reached the Condon team, Roy Craig was sent to talk to Herbert Schirmer. Craig questioned him carefully. Convinced of the law officer's sincerity, he made arrangements for Schirmer to travel to Boulder. There he was placed under time-regression hypnosis by Dr. R. Leo Sprinkle, a psychologist from the University of Wyoming. The story Schirmer told about his 20-minute period of amnesia was an utterly eerie one.

He said three humanoid creatures stepped out of the darkness beneath the space ship and approached his car. The first one had a "boxlike thing" in its hand which spread a green light all around the automobile. The other two figures moved alongside the car, one on each side. The figure on the driver's side peered in the window and stared intently, but non-threateningly at Schirmer's face. The creature had a very high forehead and cat-like eyes; it wore a hooded uniform so Schirmer could not tell if it had either hair or ears. The odd being's mouth was a narrow slit which did not move as it asked; "Are you the watchman of this town?"

"Yes, I am," Schirmer answered.

The strange visitor put its grey-white hand on Schirmer's arm. "Watchman, come with me," it said. Schirmer felt himself being lifted out of his car. He levitated with the three humanoids into the ship. "We just went z-z-z-z —like you go up in an elevator," he said.

"It was like red light inside," Schirmer continued under hypnosis. "And this big cone was spinning and there was all kinds of panels and computers and stuff. There was a map on a screen; it was a map of a sun and six planets. He said, 'That's where we're from.' He never said exactly where or anything; he just pointed at the map.

"He said the reason why they were here was to get electricity. And this sort of antenna that was on the edge of the ship kind of lifted down and extracted electricity from one of the power poles which led to the main power source there in Ashland.

"Then he said, 'Watchman, come with me,' and we went straight back down. As we walked toward the patrol car, he said, 'Watchman, what you have seen and what you have heard you will not remember. The only thing you'll remember is that you've seen something land and something take off.' And that was it," Schirmer concluded.

The policeman's tale was truly an odd one, but Dr. Sprinkle expressed his opinion that "the trooper believed in the reality of the events he described."

Saunders found the case very fascinating. "The theory of extraterrestrial visitors in intelligently controlled machines is something we *must* consider a possibility," he acknowledged. "Still, there's a lot of evidence that says there's a major psychological or psychic component to the phenomena which the vehicle concept doesn't allow for. But we don't want to put that one up as an absolute alternative either. Could there be some way in which we're dealing with a phenomenon that is *both* of these things?"

A question of that magnitude certainly could not be answered during a brief 15-month study. Fortunately, the Air Force extended the original contract for nine months more, and allocated an additional $112,000. Even so, the project was running into serious problems. There had, in fact, been many problems right from the start and the biggest of all was Edward Uhler Condon himself. The feisty man loved controversy, thrived on publicity, thought no one could tell him anything he didn't already know. He firmly believed "this whole UFO business is crazy."

His early statements to the press made his position quite clear. He was quoted as saying: "My attitude now is that there's nothing to it, but I'm not supposed to reach a conclusion for another year."

Condon was a colorful and humorous lecturer much in demand at conventions and banquets. He loved to regale his audiences with hilarious "kook and nut" cases about "goof-ohs" as he pronounced the acronym for UFOs. He read every issue of the *National Enquirer* and delighted in sending off letters demanding proof of the tabloid's silly and obviously fictional "visitors-from-outer-space" stories. He did not, however, show the slightest interest in any of the "high credibility" cases the project was examining.

In fact, Edward Condon seemed to have little interest in any of the project's research. He worked only part-time and delegated most of his authority to Robert J. Low, an electrical engineer with a master's degree in business administration. Although Condon did less work than the rest of the team, he set himself up in ivory tower luxury in a spacious, second floor office with a splendid view of the campus; he paid only rare visits to the staff's cramped offices below.

Robert Low's attitude toward the project seemed to be no more objective or inquisitive than Condon's. He always rubber-stamped his boss' decision on which cases to emphasize, which to de-emphasize and which to avoid completely. The rest of the team was beginning to wonder if their supervisors were deliberately manipulating the scientific direction of the study. Then one day, Dr. Norman Levine, a project research associate, accidently discovered something which nowadays would probably be called a "smoking gun."

Levine was thumbing through an open-files folder labeled "Air Force Contract and Background" when he chanced upon a memo written by Robert Low during August, 1966 while the University of Colorado was still considering taking on the UFO project. The memo had been sent to Dr. James Archer, dean of the graduate school, and was entitled, "Some Thoughts on the UFO Project."

In this memo, Low spelled out his feelings about the inadvisability of the university taking on such a project. "It is not respectable to give serious consideration to the possibility that such things as UFOs exist," he wrote. "One would have to go so far as to consider the possibility that saucers behave according to a set of physical laws unknown to us. The simple act of admitting these possibilities puts us beyond the pale, and we would lose our prestige in the scientific community."

Low went on to suggest a way of avoiding this embarrassment: "The trick would be, I think, to describe the project so that, to the public, it would appear a totally objective study, but, to the scientific community, would present the image of a group of nonbelievers trying their best to be objective but having an almost zero expectation of finding a saucer. One way to do this would be to stress investigation, not of physical phenomena, but rather of the people who do the observing —the psychology and sociology of persons and groups who report seeing UFOs."

Levine quickly handed the memo to David Saunders,who read it in disbelief. "The *'trick?'*" he gasped. "The *'appearance'* of objectivity? My god, Norman, we've all been had, right from the start. There's never been any *intention* of doing a real study!"

Saunders and Levine circulated copies of the memo to the other project members and their outside consultants, who also reacted with shock. James McDonald of NICAP called Low to demand an explanation, but Low hung up on him.

Shortly thereafter, Condon summoned Saunders and Levine to his office. In Low's presence, he castigated them for revealing the memo. He called them "disloyal and treacherous," and thundered, "For an act like that, you deserve to be ruined professionally!" He then promptly fired both men for "incompetence."

The next day, Mary Louise Armstrong, the project's administrative assistant, resigned in disgust, but not before telling Condon that the study was "gravely misdirected". She said she planned to go public with documentation of manipulation by Condon and Low.

"That would be highly unethical," Condon sputtered. Armstrong, finding this remark unworthy of a reply, walked out of her former employer's office.

On May 14, 1968, *Look* magazine ran a feature article detailing Condon's machinations and Low's compliance in what the magazine called "a betrayal of the public interest.... The hope that the establishment of the Colorado study brought with it has dimmed. All that seems to be left is the $500,000 trick." The shock wave created by *Look's* expose rolled all the way to Capitol Hill in Washington.

"The publication of the *Look* magazine story casts in doubt the scientific profundity and objectivity of the project being conducted at the University of Colorado," Representative J. Edward Roush (D-Ind) of the House Science and Astronautics Committee told Congress. "We are poorer, $500,000 later, not richer in information about UFOs. I am not satisfied; the American public will not be satisfied."

In the wake of his humiliating dismissal, David Saunders joined R. Roger Harkins, an investigative reporter for the *Boulder Daily Camera*, in writing a book which was subsequently published as "UFOs? Yes! Where the Condon Committee Went Wrong."

By the end of May, Robert Low had taken all the criticism he could bear. He asked to be relieved of his job as project coordinator. Edward Condon remained as unflappable as ever. He denounced his critics as irresponsible slanderers spreading "falsehoods and misrepresentations." Then as if nothing at all had happened, he went on to bring his project in on time and delivered a final report to the National Academy of Sciences, the Air Force and the general public. As expected, the report rejected UFOs as being of extraterrestrial origin.

Condon himself wrote the concluding chapter which read in part: "Further extensive study of UFOs probably cannot be justified in the expectation that science will be advanced thereby.... It is safe to assume that no intelligent life outside of our solar system has any possibility of visiting Earth."

The bulk of the 1,465-page study dealt with the psychological aspects of UFO reports, optical mirages, atmospheric electricity, electromagnetic effects and basic physics. But buried deep in the three bound volumes was a list of 23 cases classified as "unexplained." These cases were so puzzling that the committee could only clumsily dismiss them by saying they were "almost certainly natural phenomenon which are so rare they apparently have never been reported before or since."

Two of the "unexplainables" had occurred in Colorado while the study was in progress. One was a "visual" above Dry Creek Basin; the other was a "radar" at Colorado Springs. Nick Mariana's Montana sighting made the list as did Steven Michalak's Falcon Lake encounter, although no soil and rock analyses were mentioned. The Ubatuba magnesium case was tucked away in Section 111 in a chapter titled, "Physical Traces."

Officer Schirmer's experience was considered an "unexplainable," but "psychological assessment tests and the lack of any evidence left the project staff with no confidence that the trooper's reported UFO experience was physically real."

The overall tone of the Condon Report reflected Robert Low's remarks in the introductory section: "Interstellar space travel is speculation only. It is science fiction." UFO researchers and organizations such as the American Institute of Aeronautics and Astronautics went through the roof after reading the report, but most scientists and the news media accepted the project's conclusions. The report's negative impact was so great that no further serious research into the origins of UFOs was ever conducted again by a government agency.

One can only guess at how much has gone unlearned simply because one cranky old man declared further study of UFOs was unjustified. It is possible only to dream about the amount of scientific information that could have been produced by now if the Colorado UFO Project's director had instead been someone who believed the study of UFOs offered an unprecedented opportunity for the advancement of earth sciences.

If the Colorado project had insisted on further study, perhaps the mysteries that follow in this book's next chapters might not remain unsolved.

Bibliography - Chapter 10

Fuller, John G. *Look* magazine. New York. Cowles Communications, Inc. May 14, 1968.

Fontes, Olavo and Lorenzen, Coral. **Flying Saucers: The Startling Evidence of the Invasion from Outer Space.** New York. Signet Books. 1966.

Olsen, Thomas M. **The Reference for Outstanding UFO Sighting Reports.** Riderwood, Maryland. UFO Information Retrieval Center. 1966.

Saunders, David and Harkins, R. Roger. **UFOs? Yes! Where the Condon Committee Went Wrong.** New York. Signet Books. 1968.

Story, Ronald D. **The Encyclopedia of UFOs.** New York. Dolphin Books. 1980.

11

The Bizarre Death of
Snippy the Horse

Snippy was no ordinary saddle horse. She was playful and frolicsome and almost like a family pet to her owners, Nellie and Berle Lewis. The three year old Appaloosa spent her days grazing the meadows of the Harry King Ranch about 20 miles northeast of Alamosa. Each evening she would prance up to the ranch house for her evening drink of water.

On the evening of September 7, 1967, Harry King's 87 year old mother, Agnes King, saw a large object fly soundlessly over the ranch. Since she was not wearing her glasses, she was unable to tell what it was. That same evening, Snippy did not come in for her usual drink.

When the horse failed to show up the following night, Harry King grew worried. In the morning, he drove off to search for Snippy. He found the horse dead on the ground in a distant pasture not far from Mount

Blanca. The rancher nearly gagged when he saw the condition of her carcass.

Snippy's head and neck were stripped clean of all flesh; the bones, which were still attached to the body, were gleaming white. There was no blood on the ground, no scraps of flesh, hair or hide, and no tracks of any kind were near the carcass. The cut round the neck was so smooth and precise, it looked like it had been made with a scalpel.

The next day, Harry King brought Berle and Nellie Lewis out from Alamosa to view the remains of their beloved Snippy. Undoubtedly Harry felt a sense of guilt. He had been entrusted to take care of his sister's precious filly and now the animal was dead. But when Nellie saw the mutilated body, she knew there was no way her brother could have foreseen anything like this. She was, in all probability, simply glad Harry was not there when the evil deed had been committed.

The Lewises and Harry King carefully and cautiously inspected the entire area around the carcass. One hundred yards north of Snippy's corpse they noticed a flattened chico bush around which the sandy soil seemed to have been smoothed out. Nearby, Nellie Lewis found a piece of horse flesh. When she picked it up, a sticky, light green paste oozed out, burned and reddened her hand. She quickly rinsed the hand with water from a canteen and the burning ceased.

The mystified trio continued their wary exploration, stepping through the brush as lightly as soldiers in a mine field. They began finding small, circular indentations in the ground: two inches across, four inches deep and grouped in circles three feet in diameter. Each of these holes was scorched. Berle Lewis said they "looked like they'd been made by exhaust pipes."

Altogether 15 such holes were discovered within a radius of about a half-mile.

Further out, Harry King located Snippy's tracks. She had been running in the direction of the ranch house; the hoofprints clearly showed the distinctive "dig in, push out" tracks of a fast running horse. Then the tracks suddenly stopped —100 feet from the spot where Snippy's body lay.

"I'm callin' the sheriff," Nellie said with a shudder.

The Alamosa County sheriff, Ben Phillips, listened to Nellie Lewis' excited story, but he wasn't ready for a major mystery. "Aw, now Nellie, just calm down. Sounds to me like your horse got hit by lightning. Let's just let it go at that."

But Nellie Lewis was not the kind of woman who would let anything "go at that." She called all the other authorities she could think of. Each time, she got the same response: her horse must have been killed by lightning. It was not until September 23 that she was at last able to persuade a U.S. Forest Service ranger, Duane Martin, to come out and look at the dead animal.

By this time, Snippy's exposed bones had inexplicably turned a bright pink. Martin stared at the carcass incredulously. "Mrs. Lewis," he said, "This is the doggonedest thing I've ever seen. I've see stock killed by lightning but, believe me, they never looked like this."

Ranger Martin had brought along a civil defense Geiger counter. He began checking the area for radiation. Around the horse's body itself he found nothing above normal background count. But as he moved out away from the carcass, the radioactivity increased dramatically. The same was true as he walked in each direction from the horse. Snippy was encircled by radioactive soil.

At each of the "exhaust marks" and around the squashed bush, the Geiger counter again picked up unusual radioactivity. Near the bush, Nellie found a small tool of some sort which neither she nor Ranger Martin could identify. It was covered with horse hair; when she picked it up, it burned her hand just as the green paste had done.

The next day, Nellie Lewis talked to the staff of *The Pueblo Chieftain.* The newspaper soon ran an article entitled, "Dead Horse Riddle Sparks UFO Buffs." The Associated Press picked up the story. Snippy the horse became posthumously famous nationwide.

Plenty of other unexplainable things were happening in Colorado at the same time. Throughout the fall of 1967 there was a rash of flying saucer sightings between Alamosa and Denver.

On September 30, two Denverites, Dan Svoboda and his teenaged son, David, watched in awe through a telescope as a glowing, brilliantly colored disc drifted east out of the mountains. They saw it again the following night. On October 5, Superior Court Judge Charles E. Bennett, his wife and his mother, all of Denver, reported seeing three reddish-orange rings crossing the night sky. According to the judge, they were flying in a triangular formation, moving at a high rate of speed, making a humming sound.

Several Alamosa residents claimed to have seen a UFO explode in midair.

On October 8, the *Denver Post* editorialized: "In Alamosa, the theory is growing that Snippy's life was snuffed out by an occupant of a flying saucer.... The horse's strange death seems worthy of a first-rate probe. We recommend the case for top-level investigation by Dr. Edward Condon's staff at C.U. (Colorado University). With the sort of attention Snippy is getting, a convincing scientific autopsy would go far toward discrediting —or explaining the UFO phenomenon."

Not surprisingly, Edward Condon had shown little interest in the Snippy case, but other investigators were already at work. The Denver subcommittee of the National Investigations Committee on Aerial Phenomena (NICAP) had sent a four-man team to the King Ranch where they interviewed Harry King and the Lewises. The team found they were all "reliable people who are genuinely concerned, even distraught about this."

The NICAP team visited the site and took photos, soil samples, the "tool" Nellie had discovered and a "tar-like substance" from under the horse's skull. All these items were taken to Boulder and given to Robert Low, Condon's accomplice in the UFO investigation fiasco.

A person identified only as a "Denver pathologist and blood specialist" showed up at the King Ranch, offering to do an autopsy if Harry King and the Lewises promised not to reveal his name to the press. With this agreement, the pathologist sawed open Snippy's skull, expecting to find a considerable amount of fluid in the brain cavity. He found nothing. Nor did he find any fluids in the exposed spinal column of the horse's neck; Snippy's bones were as dry as any he had ever examined. When he opened the Appaloosa's carcass, there were no abdominal organs within it. Part of the flesh had turned into a gelatinous mass. This, he admitted, could have been due to the fact that the horse's body had lain out in the open for a full month.

The pathologist sent his report on to Robert Low, who was under increasing pressure from the *Denver*

Post to launch an investigation. Low decided that, rather than rely on an autopsy performed by an unidentified pathologist, he would hire someone with trustworthy credentials to examine the rotting horse.

Dr. Robert O. Adams, chief of surgery at Colorado State University's College of Veterinary Medicine and Biomedical Sciences, agreed to do the autopsy. When he had finished, he came to an odd conclusion. Dr. Adams said he found some evidence that the animal may have had a severe infection in the right flank area.

This led him to believe Snippy had run around in agony until she fell down. Then someone passing by had seen the suffering horse and slit its throat to end its misery. Next coyotes and magpies discovered the open wound and feasted on the carcass, stripping it to the bone from the withers up.

The Condon Committee accepted this explanation, but Harry King and the Lewises absolutely did not. They denied the horse had an infection; Snippy had appeared perfectly healthy when Nellie King last saw her alive. "These findings do not explain the absence of blood on the ground, or the absence of tracks –human or animal— anywhere near our horse's body," she told the Associated Press.

A lot of people throughout Colorado were also dissatisfied with Adam's solution to the mystery. One of them was Robert W. "Red" Fenwick, who wrote a folksy, weekly column for the *Denver Post.* "Old Red" came up with what he called "a simple Western explanation of how Snippy met her fate."

It was all just a gruesome prank, Fenwick wrote. "Pranksters with a yen for things eerie" had knocked Snippy down with a tranquilizer pellet from a gun. Then they hoisted the unconscious filly on a block and tackle supported by a three-pole, teepee-type rig and dipped her head into an acid bath.

The acid dissolved the horse's flesh as its bodily fluids drained out. The tripod rig caused the circles of holes found at the scene; spatterings of the acid accounted for the scorched appearance of the holes, as well as the burning sensation Nellie Lewis experienced when she picked up the oozing piece of horse flesh. As for the radiation detected by Ranger Martin's geiger counter, Fenwick noted that a sprinkling of finely ground uranium, easily available in Colorado, "would greatly enhance the element of mystery."

Fenwick's macabre hoax theory, though not totally impossible, did seem highly improbable. How could all of that been accomplished without leaving a single footprint or tire track? Why did Snippy's tracks stop 100 feet from where her body was found? How could the tranquilized horse have been moved that distance?

Each attempt to solve the puzzle only deepened its mystery. On October 12, the *Denver Post* published the results of a public opinion poll which showed its readers to be quite evenly divided between those who believed it was a hoax and those who believed it had been done by a flying saucer and those who found it completely unexplainable.

Some of the Coloradans who accepted the hoax theory swore it had been perpetrated by the Alamosa business community as a way of attracting tourists. This was an understandable reaction, for curiosity-seekers were flocking to Alamosa in record numbers; the motels and restaurants were filled every night, and so many people had trampled and littered the mutilation site that it was beginning to look like a dump ground with a dead horse in the center of it.

UFO sightings continued to be phoned in to the area's newspapers and law enforcement offices. Throughout October, pulsating red, green and white lights were seen frequently over Conejos Canyon 35 miles southwest of Alamosa, and eight sightings of soundless flying objects were made in the vicinity of Snippy's carcass.

By now, both NICAP and the Aerial Phenomena Research Organization (APRO) had completed their private investigations and evaluated their findings. Neither organization had uncovered any new evidence. Based on what their investigators heard and saw, they arrived at sharply differing conclusions.

NICAP's report stated: "Snippy's death was neither a UFO case nor especially mysterious." Their team had come to agree with Dr. Adams: Snippy died of an infection and her body was chewed on by predators. The "exhaust-like markings" on the ground were probably made by splashes of the drainage from her infection.

The Lewises indignantly rejected this explanation. "Why, it would have taken a whole herd of infected horses to make markings that extensive," Nellie Lewis told the *Denver Post.* "The extent of the markings has been verified by hundreds of people who have visited the site."

APRO agreed. That organization's investigators, James and Coral Lorenzen, also found it hard to believe that a drainage caused the exhaust marks and they added: "The most peculiar angle of the whole Snippy case was the fact that there were absolutely no tracks of any kind within the area around the horse.

"We do not say Snippy was killed by 'flying saucer people.' But we do say she died in a very strange way, and her death has yet to be explained."

And so it remains to this day; the manner of Snippy's death is still unknown. But Snippy is not the only animal to die a mysterious death on the nation's rangelands. Since 1967, thousands of horses and cattle have been found dead and mutilated in remote pastures. Although the other mutilations were not as bizarre, they were equally enigmatic.

The killings took place at night and the animal's sexual organs, rectum and udder were removed with what appeared to be very sharp instruments. Often the lips, tongues and eyes had also been cut out; usually the carcasses were drained of blood. No footprints or tire tracks were found near the butchered animals... but sometimes circular indentations similar to those in the Snippy case were found.

Over the years, hundreds of Colorado ranchers have lost livestock to mutilators. Most of them were not satisfied with the outside investigators' insistence that all this was merely the work of ordinary predators. They remained as mystified as the Lewises and fearful of whatever or whoever is out there in the night committing these bizarre atrocities.

Bibliography - Chapter 11

Associated Press, October 5,6 and 12, 1967; November 17, 1967. *Denver Post* editorial, October 8, 1967.

Fenwick, Robert W. "Red". *Denver Post*. October 11, 1967.

Howe, Linda Moulton. **An Alien Harvest.** Cheyenne, Wyoming. Pioneer Printing. 1989.

Saunders, David R. and R. Roger Harkins. **UFOs? Yes! Where the Condon Committee Went Wrong.**

New York. Signet Books. 1968.
Story, Ronald D. **The Encyclopedia of UFOs.** New York. Dolphin Books. 1980.
The Chieftain Staff. *The Pueblo Chieftain.* Pueblo, Colorado. October 7, 1967.

12

Dark Nights
& Phantom Flights

One of the most mysterious aspects of the bizarre animal mutilations in Colorado has been the frequent appearance of unidentifiable helicopters at or near the sites.

Over the past quarter of a century, law enforcement agencies across the western part of the United States have received hundreds upon hundreds of reports of unmarked, low-flying helicopters sighted and heard above the country's rangelands. Nearly always the copters were seen just before or just after mutilations occurred. In an alarming number of cases, UFOs were also seen in the vicinity at the same time.

The maneuvers of the "mystery helicopters" have been, to say the least, ominously abnormal. The choppers invariably flew at dangerously low altitudes, at levels undetectable by radar. Sometimes they behaved aggressively, buzzing witnesses and even chasing them. At other times, these phantom-like aircraft seemed furtive and zipped away as soon as they realized they were observed.

Two-thirds of the helicopters were seen and heard at night. At times these nocturnal anomalies were reported shining spotlights at the ground. On one occasion, a hovering copter in Colorado's Alamosa County flashed a light which was answered by a light from a nearby mountain peak.

One summer evening in 1975 just at dusk, a ranch family near Monte Vista spotted a red and yellow helicopter flying over a ridge with what appeared to be a "litter basket" hanging beneath it. The next day, a mutilated bull was found on the other side of the ridge. Not long after that incident, a stockman's daughter who was at home alone at the time on a remote Washington County ranch heard a helicopter approaching. She first saw it crossing a distant field at near fence-top level. The copter flew behind the ranch's main barn. As the girl hastily locked the doors, it emerged and flew directly toward the house. It came within 100 feet of the terrified youngster crouching by a window before it stopped, hovered briefly and lifted away.

In the morning, the girl's father drove out to check his pastures and found a dead, surgically butchered cow had been dropped in one of his stock ponds.

Colorado has the dubious distinction of leading all other states in the sheer number of unaccountable helicopter sightings. As a comparative example, Texas, a state more than twice the size of Colorado, logged 23 mysterious sightings during 1975, while Colorado had 72 sightings between May and December of that same year. During this period, a wide variety of types of helicopters were identified as participating in these confounding incidents. The types of craft ranged from a 2,100-kilogram, seven passenger French Alouette III to the smaller choppers commonly used by television news teams and highway patrol. Their colors ranged from white and silver to blue, green, yellow and black.

The sounds made by the rotating blades varied considerably as well. Usually the noise was the typical and unmistakable sound of a normal helicopter. But frequently the aircraft produced unusual sounds which the witnesses found hard to describe. "Soft swishings," "quiet whirrings" and "muffled rotations" were reported and contrasted to other reports of "teriffically loud" noises. At other times, the blades were said to have "whistled like air coming out of a tire."

Naturally many people suspected the U.S. military was somehow involved in these mysterious flights. Colorado's Army and Air Force bases steadfastly denied it. They insisted that their helicopters conducted all their practice and training drills on the military reservations. These aircraft only left their bases to assist in National Guard operations or to move from one base to another. Although several med-evac helicopters often fly around the state on emergency rescue calls from local sheriffs, these copters are all plainly marked with large red crosses.

Whenever the helicopters went off base, they never flew below 1,800 feet. Every pilot was required to file a complete clearance report on the destination; whenever the choppers were not in use, they were kept locked 24 hours a day.

Civilian eye witnesses who had the chance to see the occupants of the mystery helicopters all agreed that neither the pilots nor the passengers appeared to be military personnel. In fact, the occupants they saw

were almost always surrealistic, weird-looking creatures.

One of the wildest —and scariest— confronta-
tions between a rancher and the crew of a mystery
copter took place just above the Colorado state line in
southern Wyoming in October 1975.

During a two-week period from the end of
September to early October, 18 dead, mutilated cows
had been discovered in Wyoming's Uinta and Sweetwater Counties. Three more carcasses turned up in
northern Colorado. Nocturnal lights had been seen in
the sky above the ranches prior to or shortly after the
mutilations.

A Sweetwater County rancher who had lost several cattle asked to be deputized so he could have radio
contact with the sheriff's office while he patrolled the
back country. Late one afternoon, as he traveled a dirt
road, a dark green helicopter with a white patch cover-
ing its marking suddenly swooped down and flew
alongside his pickup, pacing him.

The copter was so close the deputy/rancher
could see the occupants clearly, but he could scarcely
believe his eyes. All three of them were exactly identical; young, white males with long hair, cowboy hats
and western-style shirts. They were all laughing hys-
terically.

Frantically the rancher radioed for help as he
tried to outrun the chopper. Then it zoomed ahead,
turned around to face the pickup and set down in the
middle of the road.

The rancher slammed on the brakes. He had
both a high-powered rifle and a 12-gauge shotgun on
the seat beside him; in his excitement, he inadvertently
grabbed the shotgun instead of the rifle. When he
sprang from the truck cab with the shotgun in his

hands, the copter immediately rose, swirled around and chuffed away.

Even though the rancher realized he had no chance of bringing down a helicopter with a shotgun, he blazed away at the disappearing aircraft. Later he would say he was sure he could have disabled it had he used his Mini-14 rifle to shoot out the rotor drive gears or the tail rotor. If he could have done so, the helicopter's occupants might have been arrested minutes later by a state police officer who heard the rancher's distress call. Instead, the officer could only watch as the chopper sped over him and went out of sight.

That incident was not the first nor last such harassment of people on Colorado's eastern plains. In July 1975 on Frank Fuch's ranch near Colorado Springs three girls on horseback were chased by a low-flying copter at about 6:00 p.m. At 11:00 p.m. the aircraft returned and again slowly flew over the ranch. The frightened witnesses saw a blindingly brilliant light on its underside.

Ten days later in the Elizabethtown area, two girls on foot were pursued by a helicopter until a man on horseback rode up. The chopper then flew away but was tentatively identified as a Bell Jet Ranger.

Early in August, an Elbert County youth was baling hay when he was buzzed by a helicopter which chased him all the way to his house as he fled on his tractor. The youngster ran inside, but the chopper hovered over his home for several minutes before departing.

The rural residents of Pueblo and Crowley Counties were reporting the highest number of these incidents. Several people told of having their cars chased or buzzed by helicopters which suddenly zoomed down from the sky.

On September 22, 1975, a Pueblo County rancher in a pickup was run off the road by a helicopter which then hovered directly above him. Frantically, he called for help on his CB radio. When two state police officers arrived, one of them fired a rifle at the copter and heard a ricochet. Immediately the copter flew away with the police car in hot pursuit. Then it abruptly changed directions and escaped.

Several other similar chases took place during the 1975 Colorado livestock mutilation epidemic. The longest chase began in Logan County and ended hours later in Kimball County Nebraska. It came to a sudden, mysterious halt and left many unanswerable questions.

Logan County had been heavily hit by mutilators throughout the summer. Like the rest of the Colorado cattle country residents, groups of outraged ranchers were joined by local law enforcement officers and citizens volunteers to organize a coordinated air and ground response team that could be deployed rapidly when phantom choppers were sighted.

About ten o'clock on the night of August 21, 1975, a member of a private CB group known as I-80 Control alerted the Logan County Sheriff's Office that a helicopter flying illegally low was heading across the county from the east. Sheriff "Tex" Graves, two deputies and a pilot ran at once to a private plane the sheriff had rented and took off.

They spotted the copter. With their own aircraft's running lights turned off, they followed the helicopter from a short distance. Graves radioed the chopper's location to 17 mobile ground units which were ready to join in the chase. It was the sheriff's intention to pursue the helicopter until it landed, at which time the ground units could converge upon it and arrest the occupants.

Within an hour, the copter suddenly changed course, headed northwest and increased its speed. Simultaneously, Graves received a message on his radio from two Air Force officers who told him they had been dispatched from a nearby Minuteman missile site to assist him in his chase.

The Air Force officers said their radio-equipped pickup was in continuous contact with the radar facilities at Warren Air Force Base in Cheyenne. Radar screens there, they said, were showing a second unidentified aircraft near the sheriff's plane. They urged him to circle around and look for it.

Sheriff Graves and his crew scanned the skies but saw no sign of the second aircraft even though it was a clear, cloudless night. Graves decided to stick with his original plan and continued his pursuit of the phantom copter now swishing across the Colorado state line into the Nebraska panhandle, headed in the general direction of the small town of Kimball.

Before it reached Kimball, however, it swerved off to the west into the sparsely populated rangelands beyond. Its lights went out and Graves shouted, "It's landed!"

His pilot swooped over the darkened landscape, expecting to see the grounded helicopter. It was nowhere in sight. He circled the area, flying as low as 150 feet. There was nothing below the plane —except a Minuteman missile silo; the helicopter was simply no longer in the area.

The next day, Sheriff Graves received some puzzling information. He learned from Warren Air Force Base that they had no radar system capable of tracking the helicopter or Graves' plane; Warren's only radar facilities were weather radar facilities.

Graves' first reaction was anger. He assumed

some "Air Force jokers in a pickup" had been playing games with him. Then he began to wonder if something more sinister was involved. The voice he had heard on his radio had tried to divert him away from the helicopter he was following to look for the second aircraft. Was this voice that of someone involved in the phantom flights?

Tex Graves could not answer that question, nor could anyone else.

The sightings of mysterious helicopters and UFOs continue to coincide with discovery of mutilated livestock. Ranchers, law men and concerned citizens can only speculate on what is happening on and above the prairies and grasslands of Colorado.

When attempting to find the answers, one must consider the sheer magnitude of the phenomena. Scores of different helicopters have been involved and tens of thousands of dollars in aviation fuel would be needed to keep them flying. They have to be based somewhere, and are presumably hidden between flights. Yet not one such base has ever been located.

Colorado ranchers and lawmen agreed that this means they are confronting a very big and expensive clandestine operation. Some people believe only the U.S. government would have the resources to conduct such a massive and secretive project; others think it could be the work of a multinational corporation. Some suspect it may be a combination of the two.

The motivation for such a conspiracy is impossible to determine. Perhaps the helicopter network is involved in covert biological or bacteriological experimentation. Or maybe the helicopters are not actually taking part in the mutilations, but are government aircraft monitoring the activities of the real mutilators —or diverting attention away from them. But that theory does not explain why phantom choppers are often seen at mutilation sites before the mutilations occur, nor why many mutilations are not accompanied by the sightings of helicopters.

Officially, the Federal Bureau of Investigation has declared all livestock mutilations to be nothing more than predators feeding on cattle that died of natural causes. If this is the case, why would any helicopters be present at all?

None of the attempts to explain this enigmatic phenomena are totally acceptable, let alone provable. The ultimate hypothesis, therefore, cannot be dismissed. A rather substantial number of ranchers and other night-sky watchers have come to the conclusion that these mysterious aircraft are not really helicopters at all. They are convinced the vehicles are of extraterrestrial origin, UFOs that can be transformed into objects that look like common terrestrial craft.

Admittedly that conjecture stretches the average person's imagination to the limit. But at least one Colorado resident, John Cumby of Littleton, has good reason to believe that this *is* the real explanation for the phantom flights. On Tuesday, September 23, 1975 at 7:00 p.m. he witnessed one of these transformations with his own eyes.

On that warm autumn evening, Cumby heard the sound of an approaching helicopter. He stepped to a window and saw very clearly a copter rising in the western sky. Then to his amazement, the helicopter "turned into a ball-shaped object."

His mother-in-law was in the house at the time, so Cumby shouted at her to take a look. She stepped out into the back yard where she watched the round object change into a square one with "a fluttering appendage hanging out of it." After a few moments, the

UFO vanished and then reappeared two or three seconds later at a considerable distance away. It ascended into the northern sky, shooting straight up until it was no longer visible.

Unbelievable? Not in Colorado in 1975. Incredible events were common occurrences in that extraordinary year.

But mystifying as the phantom helicopters were, even stranger things were being seen in the Colorado back country. On an isolated El Paso County ranch, phenomena were occurring which were so mind-boggling and so frightening that, to this day, they rank among the most bizarre "close encounters" in the annals of UFO lore.

Bibliography - Chapter 12

Adams, Thomas R. **The Choppers — and the Choppers: Mysterious Helicopters and Animal Mutilations.** Paris, Texas. Project Stigma. 1980. Revised 1991.

Boyne, Walter J. and Lopez, Donald S. **Vertical Flight: The Age of the Helicopter.** Washington, D.C. Smithsonian Institution Press. 1984.

Donovan, Roberta and Wolverton, Keith. **Mystery Stalks the Prairie.** Raynesford, Montana. T.H.A.R. Institute. 1976.

Jackson, Bill. *Journal Advocate.* Sterling, Colorado. August 25, 1975.

Sanders, Ed. *The Cattle Report.* Issue No. 1. Pueblo, Colorado. March, 1977.

Story, Ronald D. **The Encyclopedia of UFOs.** New York. Dolphin Books. 1980.

Stumbo, Bella. *Los Angeles Times.* August 19, 1975.

Mary Robert

13

"Something Really Scary is Going on in That Forest"

To "Jim," "John" and "Barbara," their newly purchased Colorado mountain ranch was a dream-come-true. It was a beautiful place with lush cattle pastures ringed by wooded hills. A bright, clear spring fed sparkling water into a pond near the house.

True, the house needed a lot of fixing up; it had been standing in a state of abandonment for many years. The doors had blown open and the interior was full of dirt. The electrical system needed to be rewired and the corrals needed repair. But with a little hard work, the three former city dwellers were sure they could bring their dream of a rural lifestyle to fulfillment.

Instead, their dream quickly turned into a terrifying nightmare.

Months later, when they finally decided to talk to investigators from the Aerial Phenomena Research Organization (APRO) about their frightening experiences, they insisted that their true identities be kept confidential, that their real names were not to appear in any of APRO's reports. They feared not only that they would be ridiculed, but that they would be subject to harassment by the press, the government and the military. APRO honored their request for anonymity; in all the organization's extensive reports on the investigation, the trio is referred to only as "Jim," "John" and "Barbara."

Jim was a middle-aged man who had served in the military as a public information officer. John had a background in corporate management. His wife, Barbara, was busy raising two very active children. These three close friends had pooled their financial resources to buy their Colorado dream ranch. After three months of renovations, they moved onto their new property in October 1975.

Earlier that month, on Tuesday, October 7, a tragic accident occurred on the nearby Fort Carson Military Reservation. A UH-1 "Huey" helicopter crashed in a remote ravine 12 miles south of the base's main post. Five men were killed and five seriously injured.

Public Information Officer Major Arne Anderson called the crash "the worst in the history of Fort Carson." He speculated that the 34 mile per hour winds that day may have brought the aircraft down, but he refused to say anything about probable cause until after a thorough investigation. When the probe was at last finished, Anderson told the *Denver Post* the information was classified and no report would be released to the general public; the cause of the crash "was considered to be unknown."

Although their newly acquired ranch overlooked the massive military installation, it was much later that Jim, John and Barbara began to link that "accident" to the strange events taking place on their own property.

The first of these astonishing incidents occurred while the new owners were still in the process of moving in. Jim had taken a pickup-load of household furnishings to the ranch ahead of John and Barbara. When the husband and wife arrived a short time later, they found Jim standing on the porch, leaning forward, listening intently.

"Can you hear it?" he shouted. "Roll down your windows. Listen!"

John and Barbara opened their car doors and winced as the sound hit their ears. The entire house was humming loudly, buzzing like a hive full of bees.

"Must be something wrong with the wiring," Jim said. He shut off all the circuit breakers, but the humming continued. At last it subsided and stopped. But it would return, almost on a daily basis. Sometimes it was soft; sometimes so loud conversations were nearly impossible. The homeowners never found a satisfactory explanation.

Even stranger things quickly began to happen on the ranch. One night the cattle in a pasture near the house began mooing. The watch dog, a large, normally fearless hound, started scratching at the door, wanting in. Jim picked up his rifle and went out to see what was bothering the cattle. As he walked through the nervous, milling herd, he saw a bright orange light hanging motionless in the sky a short distance away.

Jim started to approach the light but he hesitated. "If the cattle and the dog are afraid of it, maybe I should be, too," he said to himself. He left the pasture more hurriedly than he entered it.

Barbara and John's children, "Steve" and "Joe," were thoroughly enjoying their new home in the mountains. The ranch was a wondrous place to explore. They often took carefree hikes across the wooded hills, crunching through the autumn leaves beneath the now-nearly bare aspens.

One day the boys saw what appeared to be a very large bear walking through the trees on its hind legs. After that, they became considerably more cautious about where they went strolling.

On a weekend in November, Joe invited a couple of his schoolmates out to the ranch for a visit. The three friends trooped off to the nearest pasture to see the cattle. Minutes later, they came running back in a panic. They had discovered the ranch's first mutilated cow.

The adults accompanied the youngsters back to the scene where, only 200 yards from the house, the dead animal lay on its back in the fresh snow that had fallen the previous day. The cow's udder had been cleanly sliced away and removed. One eye was gone, one ear was neatly cut off. There was no blood on the snow, but there were footprints which made the group stare incredulously.

Rarely, if ever, are footprints found at mutilation sites, but these prints were extremely unusual ones. They had clearly been made by bare feet... enormous feet 18 inches long.

As everyone circled carefully around the frozen carcass, a heavy snow began falling. "Let's go back to the house," Jim advised. "Let's get the sheriff out here right away."

Jim's phone call to the local sheriff's office put him in touch with a deputy. In as calm a voice as possible, Jim described the mutilated cow and the presence of the footprints. There was a long silence on the other end of the line.

"Are you still there?" Jim asked.

"Yeah, I'm still here," the deputy said at last. "Listen, Jim, we can't send anyone out there today. This storm's going to keep us too busy. I'll come by on Wednesday. Okay?"

"No, it's not okay," Jim said a bit angrily. "We've got physical evidence here, and it's being buried by the storm."

"Sorry, Jim," the deputy said, flatly. "But that's the best I can do. In the meantime, don't go near that carcass again. Stay away from it and whatever you do, don't let those kids go back to that pasture. I'll see you on Wednesday."

Jim hung up the phone with a puzzled frown on his face. It seemed almost as if the deputy *wanted* the footprints covered up.

Wednesday came and went but the deputy did not show up. When Jim called to ask why, the officer said, "Jim, I know this is going to be hard for you to understand, but there isn't going to be an investigation of that 'mute' on your ranch. Now, before you go blowing up at me, listen. You're new here; there are a lot of things you don't know about that ranch. We need to have a talk."

"We damn sure do," Jim agreed. "I'll come by your office in the morning."

"No, Jim, don't come to the office. I'll meet you in the restaurant across the street. At five o'clock tomorrow."

The next afternoon, the totally perplexed former military man drove into town. He went to the small, nearly empty cafe where he found the deputy sheriff seated in a back booth. After Jim slid in on the opposite side of the table, the lawman leaned forward on his elbows to say, "Jim, I'm not authorized to talk to you about this, so if you ever repeat anything I'm about to tell you, I'll deny I've ever said a word to you. Is that clear?"

Jim nodded uncertainly. The deputy took a long drag on his cigaret and ground it out in the ashtray. "I know who the perpetrators of these mutilations are," he said. "Hell, every law enforcement officer in this county knows. Sheriff's department. State Police. Anybody who goes out on the back country roads at night knows. The FBI knows. And the military, they *damn* sure know."

He stopped talking while the waitress brought Jim a cup of coffee. When she left, the deputy went on in a low voice: "It's being done by extraterrestrials, Jim. And the mutilations are only part of what they're doing. I've seen things out there on your ranch that scared the hell out of me. And if you stay on that land, you're going to see them, too.

"Lights in the forest at night. And lights in the sky... big triangular lights that come down and seem to just go right into the ground. One night I was driving by your place and I saw some lights blinking at ground level off in the trees. I got out of the car and walked in a ways. There was this black box sitting there, blinking.

"I didn't want to go too close while I was alone, so

I called for back up. When my partner got there, we went into the woods together. The box was gone. It'd just vanished."

The lawman shook another cigaret out of his pack. "Something really scary is going on in that forest, but I'm not allowed to investigate it. The sheriff's got a policy, and I follow it. I file no reports about lights, or UFOs or strange creatures.

"The state police have the same policy. I'm pretty sure these directives come down from the FBI or the military. They're afraid if word of this gets out, it'll start a full-scale panic, and it probably would. But I thought you needed to know because you're living out there."

Jim pushed aside his untouched coffee. "Frankly I find this all pretty hard to believe. Sure, strange things happen on that ranch, but extraterrestrials? Come on."

"I know it sounds far-fetched," the deputy admitted. "But just think about this: that house of yours stood empty for a long, long time before you folks moved in. Why do you suppose nobody else wanted to buy it? You're living in a very dangerous place, Jim. Keep your doors locked at night." He picked up the check and left the booth.

Minutes later Jim drove off through the cold twilight headed back to the ranch. "Have I been talking to a nut?" he wondered. "Is that guy a kook? Or does he know what he's talking about?"

That evening Jim told the others about his conversation with the deputy. They, too, were skeptical. But two weeks later, John and Barbara saw their first UFO.

The two were driving into town early one morning. As they rounded a sharp curve in the road, they saw an enormous grey, cone-shaped object hovering above the trees. That afternoon, Jim discovered the ranch's second mutilated animal, a bull, in a pasture near the treeline. There were no footprints this time. Strangely, the bull was from another ranch.

Of course, Jim did not bother to call the sheriff's office. Instead he phoned a photographer friend to ask if he would come and take pictures. The photographer arrived within an hour. The two men were just about to climb over the barbed wire fence into the pasture when a large, dark shape burst out of the trees on the other side of the clearing and ran directly at them.

It appeared to be a huge, shaggy primate, running on its hind legs, making incredibly long strides through the snow. Jim and the photographer turned and fled for their lives. They did not stop running until they reached the house.

Once they caught their breath and regained their courage, Jim took his rifle out of the closet and they went back out. They retraced their frantic path to the point where the creature had stopped chasing them. They saw where it had loped away into the woods, but it was no nowhere in sight. The men walked cautiously on toward the pasture where they stared in awe at the way the fence had been torn down.

The creature had not jumped the fence, it had charged straight through it, stretching the barbed strands until they broke. There was a tuft of hair on one of the barbs, so Jim plucked it off and took it with him.

In a day or so, he mailed the hair to a biogeneticist in Denver, requesting that it be identified. When the report came back, it stated that the sample was from "no known species." The hair itself was never returned.

By now, everyone on the ranch was becoming very nervous and wary. They watched the sky and the forest constantly; Jim kept both his rifle and his shotgun within easy reach.

Late one December afternoon, he stepped out onto the front porch intending to walk to the barn. As had become his habit, he scanned his surroundings carefully before going out in the open. This time he noticed something crouched between two pines. As he stared at it, the great, hairy creature rose to its feet and stared back.

Jim stumbled to the dining room window and without turning around, began tapping on the glass. When Barbara came out on the porch, he said, "If you want to see a bigfoot, I can show you one. It's standing in the trees next to the pond."

Barbara leaned forward, using her hand to shade her eyes. As she did so, the bigfoot also leaned down and shielded its eyes with its hand in perfect mimicry. It held this pose for a few moments, then turned and lumbered away.

Throughout the rest of the winter, the ranchers continued to catch glimpses of tall, dark beasts shambling through the snow. They also frequently saw glowing discs in the sky at night, sometimes moving, sometimes hovering, sometimes descending. And they lost four more cattle to mutilators.

Early one spring evening, John and his oldest son, Joe, noticed a dim light shining from a low hill near the pasture. This particular hill had always fascinated John for there was a circular burned spot on its crest approximately 35 feet in diameter. "Let's go check that out, Joe," John said. "We should be safe if we stay in the pickup."

The father and son drove carefully up the hill and parked on the edge of the barren circle. The light they had seen from below was coming from the dark cluster of trees on the opposite side of the scorched clearing. It looked, as John would say later, "like an old car headlight." In the center of the circle there was a shiny, black box on the ground making a steady buzzing sound.

"I'm going to take a closer look," John whispered. "You stay right here, Joe. No matter what happens, don't leave the pickup."

John stepped out of the cab and entered the dimly lighted circle. When he came within four feet of the box, the buzzing instantly rose in intensity and became an angry threatening sound like something one might hear if one kicked a giant bee hive.

John dashed back to the truck. After slamming the door, he peered through the windshield to discover that both the box and the light were gone.

"They went into the ground, Dad," the boy said, astonished. "Just right down into the ground."

John drove hurriedly back to the ranch house and reported the incident to the others. Barbara put her arms around her frightened son as Jim said, "Maybe that deputy isn't crazy after all."

It was nearly midnight before everyone went to bed that night. John was still too tense to sleep. He stretched out on the davenport, gazing at the ceiling when he instinctively felt that someone was watching him. Glancing at the living room window, he saw a figure standing on the porch, looking in.

The figure was silhouetted by the yard light, so John could not see its face. But it appeared to be human; it lacked the height and stooped posture of a bigfoot. John tried to get up from the couch, but found he could not move. He was completely paralyzed.

For several long minutes, the figure stood at the window. When it turned and walked away, John found he could move again. He sat on the edge of the couch, shaking and thinking: "Whoever that was, he was letting me know he can control me. He's mad at me for trying to approach that box. This was a warning."

John double-checked the door locks even though he had a feeling that if the creature out there wanted to come in, locked doors would be no deterrent. He quietly slipped into bed beside his sleeping wife and lay awake most of the night.

In the morning, after the boys had gone off on the school bus, John told Barbara and Jim about his experience. "Just what the hell is going on on this ranch?" he asked. "We've been here for months, and we don't know any more than we did when we moved in."

Jim thought for a moment, and then said, "You know, that deputy told me the military knows all about this. I think I'll talk to some people on the base. They'll probably stonewall me, but it won't hurt to try."

The next day Jim set up an appointment to meet with one of Fort Carson's radar officers. He explained that he and his friends had seen several unidentified flying objects over their ranch and he wondered if anything had been picked up on radar.

"We have a few 'unconfirms', but I am not permitted to talk about them" the officer acknowledged.

Jim went next to Major Arne Anderson, the base's public information officer. He introduced himself as a former military PIO, described the UFO sightings and mutilations and asked what information the major had that was authorized for release.

"Carson has had its share of troubles with UFOs," Anderson admitted. "But we have directives on how to deal with them, and I have orders not to talk about it."

Jim tried to ask several questions, but the major

simply shook his head. "Sorry, that's classified," the information officer replied. Jim was about to leave when Anderson abruptly asked, "Have you had any problems with the bigfoot?"

Startled, Jim sat back down. "I didn't mention the bigfoot," he said. "How do you know about it?"

"We have directives on that, too," the officer answered. "I can't talk about it, of course, but I am concerned, because you've got a family living on your ranch. I think those creatures could be very dangerous; I wouldn't go anywhere near one of them if I were you, sir."

That evening after supper, Jim sat on the porch with Barbara and John. As they watched dusk darken the forest, he said, "Well, obviously we're not going to learn anything from either the local law enforcement people or the military. Looks like if we're ever going to find out what we're up against here, there's only one way to do it. We're going to have to deliberately make contact with whoever, or whatever, is out there in those woods.

"The next time that light comes on out on that hill, I'm going up there. Maybe that guy who was at the window last night will be there. Maybe I can let him know I want to communicate with him."

"Jim, that's crazy!" Barbara declared. "The last thing we want to do is antagonize them."

"Barbara's right," John agreed. "That 'visitor' we had was nobody to fool around with."

"But, doggone it," Jim said adamantly, "we've got to do something. After all, this is *our* ranch, not theirs."

"Is it?" John asked.

For the next few nights, Jim watched the dark silhouettes of the pines on the skyline above the circle on the hill. The planet Venus shimmered above the trees; the moon rose and crossed the night sky. Occasionally a falling star graced the darkness. Then one evening, the one light that shouldn't be there appeared again, shining balefully down from the hill. "Wish me luck," Jim said as he climbed into the pickup.

Barbara and John stood under the yard light and watched their friend drive off on the rut road that paralleled the pasture and went on up the hill. They caught occasional glimpses of the truck's headlights passing through the trees, then stop at the burned spot. The headlights went out. Several, very long minutes dragged by before the headlights came back on.

The pickup then turned around, retraced the route back down to the ranch house. Looking pale and shocked, Jim got out of the truck, embraced his friends and announced, "I think we should seriously consider moving away from here."

When they all had seated themselves around the kitchen table, Jim said, "That may have been the one time in my life when I knew *real* fear."

He said that after he parked the pickup, he saw the black box standing in the center of the clearing. Beside it, there were two humans —or at least at first glance they looked human. Jim got out of the pickup and literally forced himself to place one foot in front of the other to approach the figures. Not until he reached the edge of the circle did he see the dark shape squatting in the shadows about 30 feet away.

The bigfoot sat without moving, poised like a dog that had been told to sit and wait for its next command. Jim stopped and went no closer.

He studied the two men standing before him. They were both approximately five-foot-six inches in height and wore skin-tight, flight suit style clothing which changed colors when they moved, from brown to silver and back. They had short, blond hair, delicate facial features and extraordinarily large eyes.

One of the humanoids spoke to Jim in a monotone voice using words that sounded carefully rehearsed: "So good of you to come; there are things you must be told. We have allowed you to remain here, so far. We have interfered with your lives very little. You must not do anything that will cause us to take actions you will regret.

"You are instructed to keep silent concerning us. You will now be shown what can happen if you do not."

The humanoid gestured at the bigfoot; it rose to its full height and walked slowly toward the box. When the beast came within four feet of it, the box began buzzing furiously. The bigfoot dropped to the ground like a giant puppet whose strings had been cut.

Jim was horrified. Had they actually killed a bigfoot just to show their power? Or was the creature only stunned? He didn't wait to find out; he took a step backward. He paused and took another step back. As he carefully retreated, one of the humanoids said, "There are others here who are not like us. One of them will be coming to see you. Soon."

Jim groped his way back to the pickup and drove away as quickly as possible. After he had told John and Barbara what had happened, he added, "I don't think I want to see whatever's coming next, but I know I will."

The emotional stress the three ranchers and the two young boys had undergone during the past several months had already taken a heavy toll. The adults were chain-smoking. Everyone was edgy, jumpy, tense. Now they grew even more nervous and fearful as they awaited the appearance of something unimaginable, something they knew would be stranger than anything they had encountered so far.

They didn't have long to wait.

A few nights after Jim made his trip up the hill, he was lying on the davenport, unable to sleep. Suddenly he realized he was completely paralyzed, just as John had been. He could only move his eyes.

He glanced apprehensively at the window. As he expected, he saw an extremely bizarre figure staring in at him. Since both the yard light and the porch light were on, Jim could see the creature clearly.

It was over seven feet tall and had long, spindly arms and legs that looked almost like oversized dandelion stems. Its torso was covered by a black box from which two sets of hoses arched up to a transparent, fish bowl-shaped helmet.

The face inside the helmet was aged and wrinkled. The unblinking eyes focusing on Jim were unnaturally large, oval-shaped and totally black. For what seemed like an eternity (but was probably no more than a minute) Jim's earthly eyes locked with a pair of eyes that were utterly alien. Then the figure was gone. It didn't turn and walk away, it simply wasn't there anymore.

Instantly, Jim regained control of his body. He called out to Barbara and John. When they emerged from their bedroom, he described what he had seen and asked, "Could such a thing possibly have been real? Or was I hallucinating? Are we just imagining we see all these things?"

"No," John said assuredly. "We're not hallucinating. There are too many other people who have seen the same things we have."

Jim gazed out the window again. "Maybe it has something to do with the ranch itself. Maybe there's something here... a force or a power of some kind that causes everyone who comes here to hallucinate."

John disagreed. "Those six mutilated cattle weren't hallucinations. That torn-down fence was real, and this house does hum. We tape recorded it, remember? And what about that helicopter crash last year? We'll never know if the 'unknown cause' was UFOs, but the crash was certainly real."

"Well," Barbara sighed. "Real or not, we just cannot go on living here. We'll lose our minds." Tears welled up in her eyes as she went on to say, "I really love this place, but the time has come to leave it."

In the morning, they all started packing up their belongings.

Although the three friends' dream of an idyllic rural life had ended, they could never forget their eerie experiences. Finally they decided to tell their stories to APRO. They shared their information with reputable people they felt they could trust.

Dr. John S. Derr, an aerospace research scientists with a Ph.D in geophysics, and Dr. Ronald Leo Sprinkle, a University of Wyoming professor of counselling services with a special interest in the psychological aspects of UFO research, conducted a long series of interviews with the three ex-ranchers. Both scientists concluded that the perplexed witnesses were "intelligent, rational and perceptive individuals" sincerely seeking logical explanations for events they had seen that went far beyond their "intellectual or emotional capabilities to interpret or understand."

The APRO investigators also talked at length to several other witnesses: the photographer, the deputy and a number of friends and neighbors who had also seen inexplicable lights above the ranch. Each of these interviews matched the ex-ranchers' stories in every detail.

Jim, John and Barbara had hoped that by talking to APRO they might receive some explanations. Instead all they could be given were theories. They learned that some UFOlogists believe abnormal animals seen in conjunction with UFO sightings may be creatures abducted from other planets. Or possibly these odd beasts are the result of genetic experimentation by aliens who are creating entities capable of testing unknown environments.

Likewise, the extraterrestrials who resemble human beings could conceivably be the results of an intergalactic breeding program which mates abducted terrestrials with non-human space travelers.

It is also possible that no theory advanced so far even comes close to the truth. Perhaps UFO phenomena are far too complex and elusive for earthly scientific and physiological expertise to analyze successfully.

As Dr. Sprinkle once noted, "Traditional scientific methods don't provide 'proof' of the existence of UFOs. Nor is the evidence sufficient to determine the origins, purposes and powers of these intelligent beings. The challenge of the UFO problem is to develop our scientific and spiritual knowledge so that we can enter the "New Age" and begin to better understand this complex universe."

The planet Earth is but a small spore in this "complex universe," and Colorado is only a tiny part of this very minor planet. And yet, here in and above this state's glorious mountains, deep in its enchanted forests, and even in its grasslands, there is enough magic and mystery to qualify Colorado as one of the earth's most entrancing places.

Bibliography - Chapter 13

Bord, Janet and Colin. **Alien Animals.** London. Granada Publishing, Ltd. 1980.

Derr, John S. and Sprinkle, R. Leo. "Multiple Phenomena on Colorado Ranch." *The APRO Bulletin.* July, August, September, October, November and December, 1978; January, 1979.

Gibney, Jim. *Denver Post.* October 8, 10, 1975.

Story, Ronald D. **The Encyclopedia of UFOs**. New York. Dolphin Books. 1980.

14

Famous High Country Spook Lights

Sudden lights in total darkness are always startling to anyone who encounters them. Such illuminations can be more mysterious than shadows, and more frightening than the darkness itself.

Weird lights often appear in alpine regions in a variety of forms and intensities; Colorado's great mountain ranges are certainly no exception. Above, upon and around these mighty peaks, odd luminous phenomena frequently occur. Some of these lights can be explained; some cannot.

Mountaintops can under certain weather conditions release a corona discharge from the earth to the air, causing the peaks to glow. St. Elmo's Fire sometimes sends its cold, lambent flames forth in high altitudes creating incredible flourescences.

One of the most spectacular examples of St. Elmo's Fire in Colorado was reported in *Scientific American* in 1882. Sergeant L. M. Dey, a signal officer at the weather station on the summit of Pike's Peak, wrote that one night, the station's equipment became covered with "brushes of light."

"In placing my hands over the revolving cups of the anemometer (wind gauge), where the electrical excitement was abundant, not the slightest sensation of heat was discovered, but my hands instantly became aflame," Dey related. "On raising them and spreading my fingers, each of them became tipped with one or more beautiful cones of light, nearly three inches in length.

"The flames issued from my fingers with a rushing noise accompanied by a crackling sound. There was a feeling of a current of vapor escaping with a slight tingling sensation. The wristband of my woolen shirt, as soon as it became dampened, formed a fiery ring around my arm, while my mustache was lighted up so as to make a veritable lantern of my face."

The average person today has little chance of experiencing such a stunning phenomenon; few contemporary people stay overnight on top of 14,000-foot peaks. However, there is at least one place in Colorado where anyone can go after dark and witness some very strange and spooky lights. Appropriately, that place is a cemetery.

One mile south of the little town of Silver Cliff stands an aged graveyard where a faded wooden sign near the gate proclaims: "Silver Cliff Cemetery. Founded 1878. Famous for ghost lights reported in National Geographic."

In the daylight, this long-neglected cemetery looks anything but scary. The breeze rustles softly through the scraggly prairie grasses and crisp, dry weeds crunch beneath a visitor's feet. Not many people visit this old burial ground any more; most of those who buried their loved ones here have long since passed on themselves.

Still, as one walks through the cemetery's peaceful silence, an occasional small, sun-bleached plastic flag can be glimpsed beside a long-dead soldier's white tombstone, and pale, near-colorless plastic flowers lie in dusty bouquets on several graves.

In the oldest section, a number of the ancient stones are enclosed by rusty, wrought iron fences with creaking gates. A few of the earliest stones have crumbled and fallen down. The last remaining wooden marker is so weathered that only the name "Jeremy" is still legible.

Silver Cliff Cemetery is a tranquil, restful place... by day. But after dark, it takes on an entirely different atmosphere. This old graveyard is a *very* eerie place at night. It is pitch black and, out in that inky darkness, the "spook lights" begin to make their appearances.

The first lights a visitor will see are near the gate on the tombstone above the grave of Joseph Schmitt who died in 1929. These orange and white illuminations form a row across the reddish granite, and they are motionless. The stone has a polished surface, so it does not take long to realize the lights are reflections of the orange-tinted street lights, mingled with the white yard lights of Silver Cliff and the adjoining village of Westcliffe more than a mile away.

The other lights in the cemetery are far more difficult to explain. In fact, they seem to be completely inexplicable.

Deeper in the graveyard, beyond the Schmitt stone, a very ghostly light hangs before the Becker stone. It does not resemble the Schmitt lights in any way. It is vague and grey and its intensity varies. Sometimes for no apparent reason it becomes nearly all white; then two arm-like rays descend from it. Next it resumes its original aura-like form.

Across from the Becker stone, a similar pale, grey light emanates from a columnar tombstone but, unlike the Becker light, this faint, vertical lumination goes through no changes; it is hazy and nebulous but constant. One is led to suspect that some sort of reflection is involved since both of these stones have small, polished areas where the names and dates are engraved. But since these shiny rectangles are surrounded by rough-hewn, nonreflective granite, why does the Becker light occasionally spread down the coarser part of the stone's surface?

For that matter, what causes the Becker light to pulsate, brighten, and fade while the light from the column remains steady? This is particularly mystifying since the distant background lights never change. One must also wonder why, if these phenomena are some sort of distorted reflection, don't similar lights appear in other cemeteries with even more highly polished stones?

Odd as these lights are, it is the third type of spook light that is strangest. Throughout the cemetery, tiny, dim, white lights flash on and off, popping up and instantly vanishing. Sometimes they are no more than a quick twinkle; at other times, they seem to flit horizontally. If one attempts to approach them, they hop away remaining always out of reach. When flashlights are aimed at them, the beam reveals nothing. What causes these elusive will-o'-the-wisps?

Reflections on shiny grave stones can be ruled out. In the old section of the cemetery where there are no reflective stones, the spook lights dance in profusion. They flicker in front of the bushes and sparkle almost subliminally in the grass.

THE AUTHOR makes a daytime visit to the Silver Cliff Cemetery where the spook lights danced the night before.

Photograph by LaDonna Kutz

Once, years ago, the citizens of Silver Cliff and Westcliffe turned off every light in both towns. They they went out to the cemetery to watch the spook lights prance just as they always had. It should also be noted that sightings of the lights were reported long before these remote communities had electricity.

Moonlight is not the answer either. Some of the best observations are made on moonless nights.

In 1988, Michael White, a reporter from Greeley, accompanied an electrical engineer, Kyle Bunch, to this magical graveyard. Together, they watched the sparkling dots bounce. While both of them admitted the lights "gave the impression of having some intelligence behind them as they wobbled and danced," the two men concluded there was an obvious, natural explanation.

It was just the stars, they decided, shining down and banking their lights at glancing angles off the tombstones and into the bushes and grasses. "It is unbelievable previous investigations could have overlooked the stars' effects," they later wrote.

Bunch and White apparently did not know their theory had already been dismissed long ago. The spook lights have often been seen on overcast nights when no stars were visible. A Silver Cliff resident, Bill Kleine, used to tell of the time he and his wife saw the lights jumping about in a thick fog.

The star theory is further discredited when a simple question is asked: if starlight creates spook lights, why don't these little phantasmas flash impudently in other aged, rural cemeteries? What is so special about Silver Cliff's cemetery?

In 1969, Edward Linehan of the *National Geographic* traveled to the cemetery to marvel at the amazing lights. Like the others, he could find no explanation. He summed up the feelings of many when he wrote: "I prefer to believe they are the restless ghosts of Colorado. No doubt someone, someday, will prove there's nothing at all supernatural in the luminous manifestations of Silver Cliff's cemetery. And I will feel a tinge of disappointment."

Linehan need not worry; Colorado never disappoints anyone. Even if the mystery of the Silver Cliff spook lights is eventually solved, the explanation will probably be just as wondrous as the phenomenon itself. So it is with all of Colorado's mysteries: in this eternally magic state, if one mystery is solved and explained away, another quickly arises to take its place.

Colorado is a great, panoramic stage upon which many strange dramas have already been performed. No doubt there will be many more in the years to come. Indeed, they are surely occurring right now, this night, as the evening alpine glow fades once again from the peaks and darkness settles over this forever mysterious and miraculous land.

How to Visit Silver Cliff Cemetery

From Salida, follow Highway 291 for 30 miles to Texas Creek. Turn south on Highway 69. Enjoy a scenic 26 mile drive to Westcliffe and the adjoining town of Silver Cliff. From the western Silver Cliff city limits sign, continue 1.4 miles on Highway 69, which is also Silver Cliff's main street. Watch for Clever's Cafe & Mountain Tavern on the corner of Main and Mill Streets. Turn south at Clever's and bump carefully down the washboard road one mile to the cemetery gate. Climb over the steps and enter the darkness.

Bibliography - Chapter 14

Bunch, Kyle and White, Michael K. *The Skeptical Inquirer.* Buffalo, New York. Spring, 1988.

Corliss, William R. **Handbook of Unusual Natural Phenomena.** New York. Arlington House, Inc. 1986.

Linehan, Edward J. *National Geographic* magazine. Washington, D.C. National Geographic Society. August, 1969.

Other books from Rhombus Publishing Company:

Mysteries & Miracles of New Mexico: Guide Book to the Genuinely Bizarre in the Land of Enchantment, by Jack Kutz.
225 pages, illustrated, paperback. $7.95.
ISBN 0-936455-02-0

Mysteries & Miracles of Arizona: Guide Book to the Genuinely Bizarre in the Grand Canyon State, by Jack Kutz.
245 pages, illustrated, paperback. $7.95.
ISBN 0-936455-04-7

The Chaco Coal Scandal, by Jeff Radford.
258 pages, illustrated, paperback. $8.
ISBN 0-936455-01-2

Politics of a Prison Riot. The 1980 New Mexico Prison Riot: Its Causes and Aftermath, by Adolph Saenz.
197 pages, illustrated, paperback. $8.50.
ISBN 0-936455-00-4

To order, write to:
Rhombus Publishing Company
P.O. Box 806
Corrales NM 87048
(505) 897-3700